Is That You, Miss Blue?

An Ursula Nordstrom Book

Also by M. E. Kerr
>Dinky Hocker Shoots Smack!
>If I Love You, Am I Trapped Forever?
>The Son of Someone Famous

Is That You, Miss Blue?
by M. E. Kerr

Harper & Row, Publishers
New York, Evanston, San Francisco, London

The characters and situations in this book are fictional developments and are not meant to portray actual persons or events.

IS THAT YOU, MISS BLUE?
Copyright © 1975 by M. E. Kerr
All rights reserved. No part of this book may be used or reproduced in any manner whatsoever without written permission except in the case of brief quotations embodied in critical articles and reviews. Printed in the United States of America. For information address Harper & Row, Publishers, Inc., 10 East 53rd Street, New York, N.Y. 10022. Published simultaneously in Canada by Fitzhenry & Whiteside Limited, Toronto.
Library of Congress Catalog Card Number: 74-2627
Trade Standard Book Number: 06-023144-0
Harpercrest Standard Book Number: 06-023145-9
FIRST EDITION

For Patricia Fabry Smith
and
Elena Ninfa Mia Fabrizio
to remember the summer of '74

One

Charles School is in Virginia, and if you're ever sent there, you will need someone like Carolyn Cardmaker to warn you about it.

We met on the train.

"There's something wrong with nearly all the teachers," she said, after she convinced me to move to the rear of the train, out of sight of the chaperone. "I suppose any intelligent person would expect that," she added.

She was an "old" girl. She had spent a year at Charles School already. I had never been away from home in fourteen years, except for vacations with my family. Now I was actually supposed to live at Charles School.

"Why would any intelligent person expect there to be something wrong with nearly all the teachers?" I asked.

"Because anyone who lives at Charles School voluntarily is peculiar," Carolyn Cardmaker said. "The teacher chaperoning this train for example. Miss Blue. Have you had a good look at her?"

"We just spoke briefly at Penn Station."

"Did you see it?"

"What?"

"Never mind."

"What?"

"If you didn't see it, never mind. When you see it, you'll see what I mean about the teachers."

All the while Carolyn Cardmaker had been talking to me, I'd been envying her tan. My skin didn't like the sun, and I was as pale white as she was golden brown. I was tall and she was short; blue-eyed and she was brown-eyed. I was immaculate and proper in my new blue pleated skirt and matching blue-and-white wool school blazer. She was on the scruffy side with dozens of scratches and old mosquito bites on her arms and legs. Her skirt was navy blue cotton, which she wore with the school blazer, but the blazer was patched along the elbows and the color was frayed, the white piping torn.

She was a long-haired blonde. I was a short-haired redhead. I guessed we were both almost fifteen, because she was a sophomore, too.

I sat quietly staring out the train window for a few seconds, and then I said, "What is there about Miss Blue that I should see?"

I tried to remember my brief meeting with her by the information booth at Penn Station. All I could recall was a small bent figure in black with a nametag reading ERNESTINE BLUE fastened to the lapel of her suit, and a face wearing rimless glasses.

"What you will see is a cross," said Carolyn Cardmaker.

"A cross?"

"An enormous cross."

"She's wearing a big cross, is that all?"

"It's wearing her. It's a bigger cross than you'll ever see anyone wear, and I'm not new to wearers of crosses. You expect wearers of crosses in an Episcopal boarding school."

"You do?" That would be news to my father, who was an "unbeliever." (My mother was one, too, but I was no longer interested in any of her opinions, reactions, or philosophies.) "Unbeliever" was my aunt's word for it, and I used it myself. "Why not atheist, honey?" my father would argue with me. "Atheist is a perfectly honorable word, you know." Was it? I was never sure.

"The choir wears crosses," Carolyn Cardmaker continued, "and Reverend Cunkle wears one. Some of the faculty wear them, a few students wear them, and Miss Blue is worn by one. You'll be seeing a lot of crosses, don't worry."

The train was racing toward the beginnings of Washington, D.C., where we would change for another train. I shut my eyes and remembered my father, smelling of pipe tobacco and good leather, hugging me at Penn Station and promising, "Next week I'll leave for Washington, and the week after that we'll be set up in Maryland. You can come for weekend visits. It isn't as bad as you think, sweetheart."

Carolyn Cardmaker sighed and said, "Do you know what Miss Blue calls Jesus? She calls him her buddy. She sings that old song 'My Buddy' and she says it makes her think of Jesus. She can hear Jesus. Far out."

"What do you mean she can hear Jesus far out? Far out where?"

"I mean it's far out that she can hear Jesus. It's Ding-A-Ling City."

"Weird," I agreed.

"I hope you're not too religious."

"I wasn't raised to be," I said, which was an understatement. I'd only been to church once in my life, for my Grandmother Deacon's funeral last spring. Both my mother and father had attended with me, neither one standing with head bowed during prayers but staring straight ahead at the white coffin (closed) with the roses on top, about a dozen pale red ones.

You might say that was my mother's and father's last public appearance together. About ten days later my mother took off for New York City, where she was going to join Bobby Santanni. He was fourteen years her junior, and he was attending New York University, where he was studying for a Ph.D. in Psychology. My father had hired Bobby last summer as a research assistant. He was tall and skinny. He smoked a pipe and was as good as an encyclopedia for quick information, and there was a certain conceited air about him.

My father kept asking me if I wanted to call my mother before it was time for me to get my train to Charles School. I didn't want to. I might have been able to take her just running off like she did, but I didn't think I'd ever get over her running off with Bobby.

Ever since my grandmother's funeral, one of the hymns had kept coming back to me; not the whole thing but just a few lines of melody and the words: *The night is dark, and I am far from home; Lead thou me on: Keep thou my feet; I do not ask to see The distant scene; one step enough for me.*

"If you weren't raised to be religious, why did you get shipped off to an Episcopal school?" Carolyn Cardmaker brought my mind back to the present.

"Because my father is in business in Maryland, and Charles is nearby. And I had an aunt who went to Charles. She said the religious thing wasn't emphasized."

Carolyn Cardmaker shrugged. "It's not played down, either. We have chapel every single evening. We go to church twice on Sunday. We have Bible once a week. And we have Miss Blue, who can hear Jesus."

"Why did *you* get shipped off to Charles?" I asked her. She wasn't at all my idea of a boarding-school girl. She didn't look like any of the girls in the Charles School catalog, either. She was very short. She was not one of those all-American beauty types in sports clothes, pretending to be woodsy in the fall or beachy in the summer. She sat with her legs all caught and curled around each other like a contortionist, and her elbows jabbed into my sides periodically when she made a point. Her fingers were short and stubby, and she had several hangnails.

She said, "I'm a P.K."

"What's that?"

"A Preacher's Kid!" She was tracing the initials PK in the soot of the train window with her finger. "I'm a preacher's kid with a high I.Q., which means I won a scholarship. There are only four reasons why anyone is ever shipped off to Charles School, and I qualify as a Number One. Number One is Bright and Pitiful. I could be Bright and Black, or Bright and Oriental, or Bright and a Migrant Worker's Daughter. But I'm worse than all of those because I'm bright and a preacher's kid, which means that I'm practically a pauper. I'm even wearing a secondhand school blazer."

"I thought Charles School wasn't for rich people, anyway," I said. "My Aunt Helen said it definitely wasn't."

"It isn't a school for poor people, either," Carolyn Cardmaker said. Then she looked me over thoughtfully. "I don't know what number *you* are yet, but Flanders is a funny first name. You probably have at least one eccentric parent. One eccentric parent can cause plenty of problems, so you may be a Number Three."

Our last name was Brown, so both my parents had wanted something less ordinary for my first name. I was Flanders Dunbar Brown.

"I'm not a number anything," I scoffed. "I told you my father's starting a new business in Maryland. There's not room for me yet."

"You're a Number Three, I was right," said Carolyn Cardmaker. "The Number Threes are In the Way."

The train whistle blew a shrill greeting to Washington.

I said, "I probably won't even finish the term," forcing a casual air. "My father will probably be sending for me as soon as everything's set up."

It wasn't the truth, but neither was it the truth that I was a Number Three. At least I didn't think it was.

I hadn't changed Carolyn Cardmaker's mind. "Definitely a Number Three," she said. "But it could be worse. You could be a Two or a Four."

"You can't fit everyone into a slot like that, Carolyn."

"Don't call me by my first name. Everyone calls me Cardmaker."

"You can't, Cardmaker!"

"You can at Charles. At least about this you can, I promise you. If you're at Charles, you're either 1) Bright and Pitiful, the scholarships; or 2) On the Ladder, the social climbers; or 3) In the Way; or 4) Out of the Ordinary!"

"I'm Number Five," I said.

"What's that?"

"A new category," I said. "It's called Not Any of those Things."

Cardmaker continued, blithely ignoring my remark. "A lot of the people you'll meet are On the Ladder. *They* aren't, really, their parents are. A good boarding school is part of the image social climbers like to create. The parents can sit around the country club while the waiter shakes up martinis and they can let it drop that little Ann-Babette is off at Charles School, you know, très chic."

"Not très chic if they're shaking up martinis at their country club," I said. My father always stirred his very gently. Remembering his advice concerning martinis, I said, "You never shake a martini. You could bruise the gin that way."

Cardmaker's face became red with humiliation. She reached down on the floor of the train for a huge patent-leather bag. The straps were worn and the patent leather was peeling. She began rifling through it as she talked. "Okay. Okay. P.K.'s don't know a lot about martinis. In their formative years they were being instructed to death in manners and not cocktails, which is why half of them go bad and end up on the police blotter or somewhere worse like Charles School. . . . Oh, some lucky P.K.'s get to learn that stuff. The real high Episcopalians with the ten-dollar incense and the fancy-schmancy parishes in Richmond and Philadelphia and New York City, but not us pitifuls from the sticks in Outer Mongolia, which is what it's like where we live in Pennsylvania. Men drop dead out in front of their houses all winter long trying to dig out. They suffer heart attacks. Winters the snow goes past our downstairs windows. Winter mornings our living room is as dark as night."

Cardmaker was still poking around inside her bag.

I said, "I used to live in Upstate New York, not far from where you live. We never had snow past our downstairs windows. Our living room was never as dark as night in the morning."

Cardmaker didn't bother to acknowledge my remarks.

"There's something I want to ask you, too," I said, losing a little of my feeling that she was an authority figure of any kind just because she knew Charles School and I didn't. "What are Out Of The Ordinarys?"

"The Number Fours?" she said. "They're flawed in some way. You'll see them right away if we have any aboard this year. There was a dwarf in the class of 1957. She's a psychiatrist now in Atlanta. Two years ago there was an albino from Jackson, Mississippi. She had to wear dark glasses and put up black shades over all the windows. She couldn't take gym, either, or stay outdoors longer than three and a half minutes."

"You're right," I said. "I'd rather be a Number Three."

"You're probably more of a Three than you even know,"

said Cardmaker. "Most Number Threes are."

"Thanks," I said. "It's nice to have a vote of confidence."

"Anyway, in the beginning everyone feels like a Number Three," said Cardmaker, removing a package of Chesterfields from the bottom of her old shoulder bag. "Being shipped off to Charles is a lot like being shipped off to an asylum, you know? I don't mean just the fact the teachers are all strange. I mean getting used to the food and certain grotesque things they put in the food to curb our sexual appetites, and the fact there aren't any private johns and the bells ring out commands all day. Stuff like that."

I couldn't think of anything to say. I had an impulse to repeat the line from the hymn played at my grandmother's funeral, to say something like, "Cardmaker, I do not ask to see the distant scene; one step enough for me," but I lost the energy it took to be amusing. It had gone with whatever high spirits there might have been tagging around, left over after breakfast early that morning with my dad.

Cardmaker said, "I've been dying for this all day," scratched a match, and lighted her cigarette.

"Is smoking allowed?"

"*Verboten!*" said Cardmaker with a thick German accent. "Eef I am deescovered I vill be kaput!"

"Aren't we practically in the station?"

"Practically. That's why I'm sneaking this now. It'll be the last chance before we change trains. On the next train there'll be more girls and another chaperone, no way to sneak a coffin nail."

She blew out some smoke rings, turned to me, and said,

"How did you get the name Flanders?"

Her smoke poured past my face and I waved it away with large, exaggerated, hinting gestures. It did no good. Cardmaker was not easily thrown off posture.

I said, "My mother and father were fans of a doctor who lived years and years ago named Flanders Dunbar. She believed that all physical diseases were rooted in your particular emotional problem. If you had a lot of gall," I said, fanning smoke from my eyes, "you could get gallstones."

"Psychosomatic medicine," said Cardmaker.

"Flanders Dunbar was a pioneer. My folks wanted to bring her research up to date." After that period there was the handwriting analysis phase, then a lot of encounter stuff, and then this new primary therapy, with Bobby coming from New York to assist. One day I heard him call my mother "Tutta." I asked him what it meant and he said it was just something in Italian. I asked him again what it meant, and he said, "It means 'all,' 'everything,' " and he laughed and looked very embarrassed and said, shrugging, "It just means she's the boss."

"You said your father was in a new business?" Cardmaker said, blowing out three perfect O's.

"Don't you think smoke rings attract attention?" I said. "What if Miss Blue turns around and sees smoke rings over your head?"

"She won't turn around," Cardmaker said. "She knows I'm smoking."

"She does?"

"She does."

"Then she's neat."

"She's gutless," Cardmaker said. "She's afraid to make waves."

"I see," I said, glad we were no longer pursuing the subject of my father's new business. Of all of their schemes, I hated Attitudes, Inc., the most.

Cardmaker took a drag from her cigarette, inhaled, and endured a brief coughing fit which left tears in her eyes. She was stalwart. She continued as though nothing had happened, speaking with hoarse difficulty. "Have you ever heard of John Cardmaker, Flanders? He's my great-great-great and keep going back for eons great-grandfather."

I shook my head no.

"No one has, but they should have. Just because he didn't cotton to the idea of the Pope and all the pomp and circumstance, do you know what the church of Rome did to him in 1553?"

I said, "I know very little about that sort of thing, Cardmaker."

"That's why I'm telling you. You can research it in *Fox's Book of Martyrs* if you doubt my word. First they burned a man before John Cardmaker's eyes, practically on top of him, and then they asked John Cardmaker to recant. But he didn't, Flanders. He went across to the stake and kissed it. Then he died a fiery chunk of charred flesh with the people yelling, 'Lord strengthen thee, Cardmaker!'—because the people were proud of his courage!" She tapped the tip of her cigarette and a long ash fell into her lap. She rubbed it into her skirt until it no longer showed. "So now you know a little about my ancestry," she said.

I said, "That story, or the cigarette smoke, or the whole idea of going to Charles School is making me feel sick."

"Religious people are always burning other religious people," said Cardmaker, ignoring my queasy feelings. "There's a whole history of it. It's still going on, too. In Indochina, in Ireland. Religious people are often grotesque."

I had never admitted it to anyone, but I did believe in God. Was that being religious? I wasn't wearing out my knees at the side of my bed every night, but I did say my own version of prayers.

"WASHINGTON, D.C.!" a porter yelled as the car door swung open and he strode through. "WASHINGTON! WASHINGTON!"

Cardmaker waited for him to pass and studied her cigarette between her fingers. "I've almost made up my mind that I might not be religious myself," Cardmaker said. "Want a drag before I kill it?" I rejected the offer.

Cardmaker continued, "The trouble with giving up God at this point in my life is that you really need someone higher up when you're stuck at Charles." She looked across at me. Smoke was curling up past her face. "Wait until you meet APE."

"Who's Ape?"

"Who's APE?" She laughed knowingly. "She's the headmistress. Annie P. Ettinger. . . . Oh, you don't know the half of what awaits you, Brown. Lord strengthen thee." She dropped her cigarette and squashed it with her shoe.

I said, "Amen," aloud, for the first time in my life.

Two

All the residence halls at Charles School were named after Charles Dickens novels. Cardmaker had warned me about it.

"Miss Charles, the founder, was an Anglophile," she'd told me. "It'll show up in a lot of ways, like we call the john the W.C., and there are all sorts of queues: The Sweet Shoppe Queue, the Mail Queue, et cetera, and there are pictures in the parlors of kings and queens and moors and palaces."

My room was on Little Dorrit hall.

Before I was given this information, I had to locate my luggage, be assigned class cards, and sit through "Preliminary Welcome," which was a lecture on the traditions of Charles School. (It was traditional, for example, to attend classes on Saturday and have Mondays off. I wondered if that was an English custom, an Episcopal one, or a Southern one. Cardmaker had said the traditions were usually one of those three.)

When I finally left the registration line, I saw Cardmaker waiting for me. She roomed on Hard Times with another sophomore. She had already unpacked and made her bed and gossiped with her roommate while I was going through orientation.

"Where are you living?" she asked.

"Little Dorrit."

"There's been a mistake, Flanders."

"No, that's where I'm going to be."

"There are only single rooms on Little Dorrit," Cardmaker said. "No one rooms on Little Dorrit."

I said, "I do. I have asthma."

"So what! You don't want a single on Little Dorrit. Believe me!"

"I'd keep a roommate awake."

"So what!"

I kept arguing in favor of the single by describing my worst symptoms: difficult respiration, livid countenance, cold extremities, coughing with expectoration; and Cardmaked kept replying "so what" after every one. We were walking up the stairs of Old Main and down past David Copperfield, in the direction I'd been told to take to Little Dorrit.

"Apply for a change immediately," Cardmaker said. "Do you know what goes on on Little Dorrit all day long and half the night?"

I knew from experience there was no way to stop Cardmaker from telling me. I could see the dark blue beginnings of evening from a hall window, and I realized I'd been in Cardmaker's company nearly twelve hours, counting the wait in Washington, D.C. . . . The single sounded good to me suddenly.

"They practice piano on Little Dorrit," Cardmaker said. She had changed her clothes. She was wearing a pair of boy's black cotton pants a size larger than she was, with the legs cut to shorts, and a black-and-white T-shirt with a fancy insignia stamped on it in gold. Across the T-shirt was written: *Cadet Butler Peabody, Wales Military Academy, Wales, Virginia.*

She had told me about Peabody on the train. He was a P.K., too. They had worked up some kind of agreement between them whereby Cardmaker would be asked to all the W.M.A. social affairs, and Peabody would be invited to all those at Charles School. Cardmaker said it was a practical arrangement worked out in contract form by Peabody, who was going to Harvard eventually to study law.

Cardmaker continued to denigrate Little Dorrit as we walked there.

"They practice piano, violin, trumpet, whatever anyone around here plays," she said, kicking at imaginary stones in her path with her ragged sneakers. "Little Dorrit is a practice hall, that's why the rooms are so tiny, Flanders! All they do is move out a piano and move in a bed! It was never supposed to be a residence hall! There isn't even a faculty chum assigned to Little Dorrit, and every other hall has one!"

"I don't care, Cardmaker," I said. I didn't either. In my mind I was writing letters to my father, suggesting ways I might be of help in running Attitudes, Inc. I had sunk that low in less than a day.

"Wait, it gets worse," Cardmaker promised. "Do you know who they always put on Little Dorrit? Number Fours! Always! You're liable to room next door to a pinhead."

I just kept repeating "I don't care" over and over in a voice softened by severe doubt that I would ever be happy again.

"Do you want to share a bathroom with a pinhead?"

We stepped three steps down to Little Dorrit, and the question went unanswered. It was quiet there. No one was dragging trunks and suitcases by. There were no open doors with views of twin beds piled high with blankets and sheets, and girls flocking about getting acquainted. There was no one there but Cardmaker and me.

I said, "I'm in 7."

"I hope you're not going to be the only one on the hall," said Cardmaker. "There *have* been years when there weren't any Number Fours in the school."

"I'd just as soon be spared washing up next to a pinhead," I said.

"And spend the night alone on this hall?" Cardmaker said. "I wouldn't spend the night alone on this hall for anything! This hall is isolated from the whole school—that's why it's okay to play instruments up here. You could play a tuba or holler bloody murder, and no one would hear."

A voice behind us said, "Someone would hear, Carolyn."

We turned around. I remembered the woman. She was not much taller than Cardmaker. She was thin and gray-haired, with bright blue eyes behind the rimless glasses and very pale white skin. She was dressed in black, with an enormous silver cross hung about her neck.

"You didn't ride with the rest of us today," she said. There was a heady scent of gardenia attached to her, and her teeth were very white. "But we met at Penn Station, remember?"

"How do you do again," I said, putting out my hand to shake hers. At "Preliminary Welcome" I was told that it was traditional to shake hands with faculty members when greeting them for the purpose of conversation.

"I've been waiting for you," she told me. She received my hand and for a very quick moment gripped my fingers viselike, then let go. She dropped her hand to her side and wiped her palm against the side of her dress. "I'd stepped around the corner to admire the painting of Mary, Queen of Scots, at the top of the staircase. It's my favorite painting."

My own palm was wet from its encounter with hers.

Cardmaker spoke up then: "If someone *were* to play the tuba, or more likely, scream bloody murder up here all by herself, how *would* someone hear?"

"Carolyn," said Miss Blue. "Oh, Carolyn. I prayed so much for you this summer."

"How would someone hear?" Cardmaker persisted.

"Someone around that corner," said Miss Blue, pointing to the left of the Little Dorrit sign, "with very excellent hearing, thanks to our Lord, would most definitely hear. . . . And I would be down here in the wink of an eye."

"You mean they've made a faculty room on David Copperfield?" said Cardmaker.

Miss Blue smiled and nodded. The huge cross bobbed against her bosom, which was surprisingly ample for such a small, thin woman, and very firm for someone her age. How old was she? I was never good at telling ages—my own parents always looked so young. I guessed she was fifty-five, maybe even sixty.

Cardmaker said, "The only room on David Copperfield is the old linen closet and utility room."

Miss Blue's cross bobbed again in agreement.

I was holding my breath, fearful that Cardmaker would make some awful crack about putting Miss Blue in a closet to live. Without even knowing her, I sensed she needed protection. Then, and in the future, I would hold my breath when I came upon Miss Blue coping with others, or attended her classes, or just watched her from a distance in church, at chapel, in places where she was most vulnerable. And I would never forget the viselike grip, the strength of it and the willfulness.

Miss Blue was reciting from memory, a section from the faculty rule guide. "Any residence hall with two or more girls living on it has assigned to it a faculty chum." She smiled up at me, that strange smile of hers, almost pristine, as though it were the first time she had ever asked her face to try that gesture. With an accompanying flush to her skin, she said to me, "I'm yours."

Cardmaker didn't give me a chance to reply. She said, "Two or more, two or more. Then there'll be more on Little Dorrit, or two? How many will there be on Little Dorrit, Miss Blue?"

"Another besides Flanders," said Miss Blue. "A Miss Agnes Thatcher from Birmingham, Alabama. Due any time now."

Three

I never thought I'd find myself doing one of the Attitudes, Inc., exercises on my own. I have a thing against any philosophy or "ology" my father gets wrapped up in. My father was once described by an ex-boyfriend of mine as the answer to the question: What does the duck say? (Quack, quack, quack.) He didn't know it while he was making the crack, but that was our last date. Love me, love my old man.

But I have to admit Mr. Teddy Brown does things sometimes even I wonder if he really believes in. Like Attitudes, Inc., this new sort of therapy farm he was setting up in Maryland. How was my father going to help people solve their problems with therapy when he wasn't even a Ph.D., much less a real doctor? His answer to that was that the world was expanding beyond the confining concepts of doctor/lawyer/merchant/chief, and people were discovering corruption and narrowness in the old sacred-cow authority figures. He said people wanted less commercial, more creative leaders.

But he wasn't doing it for peanuts himself. Every "seeker" paid $150 per weekend, and had to sign for a minimum of six. (I can remember when my mom and dad were doing handwriting analyses by mail order for fifty dollars apiece.)

Anyway, my second twilight at Charles School, as I was stretched out on my bed listening to someone across the hall practice the piano, I thought of the P/N exercise, which is an elementary Attitudes, Inc. exercise. Here's how it works. You shut your eyes and you see a perfectly blank white screen.

On the left side you write POSITIVE.

On the right side you write NEGATIVE.

Then you draw a line down the center, separating P from N.

You're ready now to list the positive and negative aspects of your present situation. You must list a positive before a negative, and you cannot list more negatives than positives and vice versa, though they don't all have to be really heavy aspects.

For example, my first positive was:

I'm lying down.

This is how my P/N exercise took shape:

POSITIVE	**NEGATIVE**
I'm lying down.	The food is awful and it's supposed to be loaded with saltpeter to keep us from getting horny and turning into dykes or running off with WMA cadets.
Cardmaker will be a good friend.	No sign of Agnes Thatcher so far and there are rumors that she is not coming, or that she came but was discovered to have both male and female sex organs and was sent back home. . . . It is a little spooky being the only one on the hall.
I met a teacher I liked named Miss Horton. She is the librarian.	I met APE, not personally but at Morning Assembly, and she is as bad as Cardmaker said she is. She looks like an old mud turtle which someone has stood upright and put a dress on. She wrote a sentence across a blackboard that she said she wanted us all to memorize. It was: SIMPLICITY IS THE KEYNOTE OF REFINEMENT. She broke her piece of chalk with the strength it took to write it. Cardmaker said a mild way of describing her is "very excitable." Cardmaker says a little man will appear at her table evenings, who is Billy Ettinger, her husband (!).

I like Cardmaker's roommate, Cute Dibblee, too.

There is a breeze from the window.

No asthma attacks so far.

My room is not only on the practice hall but directly under the large tower with the bell inside which triggers all the activity around this place. It is a horrible, large **clang** and then a great **dong dong**. CLANG (pause) DONG DONG. I lie here wondering how it is possible to **hate** a **bell**.

My room isn't much bigger than a closet and I have to share the W.C. with Miss Blue. It's very unusual to share a ~~john~~ W.C. with a faculty chum, but Little Dorrit isn't typical. . . . Miss Blue has put in a nail near the mirror—to hang what on?

There is a dance coming up and it is actually formal. **Formal!** I am expected to wear that long dress we were required to bring! Cardmaker says the reason it is formal is because at get-acquainted dances, the cadets often try to smuggle in booze. Formal dresses are supposed to remind us we are ladies, and we do not drink booze no matter how nervous and self-conscious we are. A long dress makes everything more difficult, too, Cardmaker says. . . . The cadets have to wear full-dress uniforms.

Five more days till Monday and a chance to go to the movies in town.

The reason we get Mondays off instead of Saturdays is that on Saturdays the streets of Wales are filled with cadets and high-school boys and other attractive people. Mondays there is no action whatsoever in the city but troops of little goody girls in their blue wool blazers being herded off to the movies or shopping with an honor senior in charge.

That was as far as I got in my P/N exercise before the old CLANG—DONG DONG signaled dinner. (According to my father, P/N keeps you from being repressed as well as forcing you to think positively. All I know is I never did that exercise when the P's came out longer than the N's.)

I had ten minutes from CLANG—DONG DONG to get myself cleaned up and down to Dombey and Son Dining.

From my bedroom window I could see a lot of the faculty pouring out of the house trailer next to the tennis court. It was the only place at Charles School where smoking was permitted. It was called The Caravan, and only faculty members were allowed there.

I'd heard Miss Blue never went near The Caravan, not just because she didn't smoke, but also because she didn't mingle; she was a loner, not exactly by choice. She had the effect on most people of embarrassing them, as in the sentence "I was embarrassed for her." If Miss Blue wasn't in her room, and she rarely was, she was down by the staircase off David Copperfield, sitting there in the straight-backed wooden chair, reading the Bible or staring up at that painting of Mary, Queen of Scots. I guess the linen supply closet wasn't much bigger than my room; maybe she was claustrophobic. I only knew she spent a lot of time in that chair in the hall, and it was not the kind of chair anyone's body would look forward to being lowered into. I don't think it had been put at the top of the staircase with the idea anyone would ever want to sit in it. It was just old and hard and handsome, as good a decoration as any, not there for creature comfort.

That night she was neither in her room nor down the hall. As I tried the bathroom door she called out that she was sorry, she would be out in a moment.

I was ready to skip washing my hands and proceed to Dombey and Son Dining when the lock on the door rattled and Miss Blue came out. She was blushing as usual, and her eyes were blinking fast, as usual, but something about her attitude was different, and she was even pausing a moment as though she might be capable of conversation, instead of scurrying past me around to David Copperfield. I hoped she hadn't decided she was capable of conversation, because I had already perceived that she was the kind of adult I could never think of anything to say around. She was the sort I wanted never to be left alone with, the sort whose eyes I could never meet with my own, the sort who left me totally speechless, unable even to cough up the minimal civilities like it's such a lovely day out, isn't it, or something about drought, rain, snow, sunshine, *something*.

My father always says that when you're shy you should ask a question, but I don't know why he thinks that's such a splendid solution, since the question itself isn't that easy to think up. He claims people love to answer questions, especially directions to places. "It's the kind of question you ask that's important," he says. "Don't ask anything personal, but ask, for example, how to find someplace you know they can locate easily. It makes people feel good to direct you. Or ask if there's a restaurant nearby they could recommend, or if there's a recent book that's amusing...."

But I didn't have to think of a question because Miss Blue asked me one.

"Have you seen the new addition, dear?"

"Agnes Thatcher? Has she arrived?"

"Oh, no, dear. Not Agnes Thatcher. Jesus. In the bathroom."

For a moment I had forgotten the nail with nothing hanging on it. I stood there, unsure of how to proceed.

"Next to the mirror," said Miss Blue. "I put Him there. You don't mind Him there, do you, Flanders?"

"Of course not," I said.

"You may tell me if you don't want Him there. After all, we share the bathroom."

I was grateful that she didn't call it the W.C. I still preferred bathroom, even john, even can or head, to W.C. W.C. sounded so affected for a place where affectations wouldn't do you very much good.

I said, "I really won't mind, Miss Blue."

"You may take a peek at Him."

I went inside the bathroom and looked up where the nail used to be.

There hung a picture of Christ, one of those crown-of-thorn types showing mostly His head, with some drops of red blood on His face.

There was a verse under His face:

> O bleeding face, O face divine,
> Be love and adoration thine.

Miss Blue was standing behind me, her hands folded across her chest and resting against the huge silver cross. I could feel the tiny blue bird-eyes watching the back of my head, waiting for me to turn and say something.

I knew if anyone else my own age had been there we'd have had a giggling fit and collapsed on the floor. Not that the idea of Christ's bleeding face was funny, but things out of context often seem preposterous. And someone like Miss Blue, for all her serious intentions, comes off crazy as a loon. But if you're confronting the thing alone, as I was confronting alone Miss Blue's addition to our bathroom, instead of getting hilarious, you get self-consciously aware of how little you can respond: You want out.

That's what I wanted—O U T.

"It's fine, Miss Blue."

"The little poem is so expressive."

"Yes."

"I have always felt special about the word 'adoration.'"

"Yes?"

"Adoration."

"It's a neat word," I said uncomfortably, stupidly.

She looked at me as though I had said something very profound. She thought a moment. "Yes," she said. "Yes, it is neat. Neat. From the Latin *nitere*: to *shine*."

She was looking up at me, nodding her head in the

shaky way she had of nodding her head so that you weren't sure that she was doing it voluntarily. Did she have the shakes, or did she want to nod her head?

I couldn't cope.

"I'll be late for dinner," I shouted over my shoulder as I ran from the bathroom and down the hall.

I wished I'd said "we." I wished I'd waited and walked with her to Dombey and Son Dining.

But I resented it, too, that this woman had been foisted on me, that I was going to have to contend with her for a long time. And I knew that the way I'd bear it would be to make it all a joke, one big laugh to share with everyone.

I began immediately that night in the dinner line.

Four

Before we could enter Dombey and Son Dining, the faculty had to precede us, and APE and her husband, Billy, had to precede the faculty.

That night was my first look at Billy. He didn't appear at every meal. According to Cardmaker, sometimes he was served in his room on a tray, because he had a bad heart.

Even though the floors leading to Dombey and Son were carpeted, you could hear APE coming—or maybe it was more that you could feel it, the way you could feel distant thunder some quiet summer nights. There was a very subtle rumbling, and then came this tortoise face with glasses on, and great dewlaps held in check by a choker of pearls, the head framed by this very wiry gray hair, brown eyes staring out coldly as if their own little message was: Don't try to get any sympathy out of *me*!

APE was a large woman in every way, not fat, but big. Her legs were long and thick; she had a huge rear end; a grand bosom; long, broad shoulders, and great hams for upper arms, with flabby poles connecting them to large hands with long fingers and manicured short square nails. On her wedding finger she wore a gold band with a large round diamond. Cardmaker had warned me that she rubbed the diamond whenever anger was building up inside of her.

Bouncing along behind APE that evening was this little man, almost doll-like by comparison; a sweet-faced, pink-cheeked, bespectacled old fellow with a few hairs combed across his bald head. He was not an inch taller than five feet. Cardmaker told me he bought all his clothes in Saks Fifth Avenue's Boys' Department. He was very well groomed in this little pin-striped suit with a vest, and across the vest was strung a gold chain with a Phi Beta Kappa key hanging from it. Cardmaker said he did the Sunday *New York Times* crossword puzzle in full, every Sunday morning at breakfast, with a pen!

Although APE went past most of the student body and faculty on this short trek into Dombey and Son, it was not her custom to notice anyone. I suppose she figured it would be awkward to trudge along saying hello hello hello hello hello hello et cetera, so she simply marched ahead looking neither to her left or right.

Billy looked left and right. He smiled, winked, nodded. He was like some merry little court jester following the old queen mother. Cardmaker said they shared the same bed, in a huge suite on Tale of Two Cities. She said I could see their windows from my room on Little Dorrit; the two long ones with a small balcony in front belonged to the bedroom, the other three were the sitting room and his study.

After APE and Billy went into the dining room, the faculty filed in. I turned my back on this scene because I didn't want to face Miss Blue again. While we stood there, I told Cute Dibblee and Cardmaker about the picture of Jesus on the bathroom wall, with the inscription underneath.

We all cracked up.

"What table are you bleeding faces headed for tonight?" Cute asked.

"O face divine, let's try Miss Horton's," I said.

If you wanted to sit with anyone in particular, you had to agree ahead of time whose table you were aiming for. Each table was headed by a faculty member. There were a few teachers no one ever raced to sit with, and guess who one of them was. For one thing she always wiped her hands on her napkin after she passed anything anyone else had touched; for another, there was this strong scent of gardenia about her. Who wanted to eat corn fritters or mashed potatoes or meat loaf or chicken à la king enveloped in the smell of gardenia?

But the worst thing, from my point of view, and even from Cardmaker's, who should have been more blasé about such matters, was trying to keep a straight face when Miss Blue said grace. Where most teachers were concerned grace was something like "OLORDWETHANKTHEE FORTHISFOOD," mumbled in about six seconds, after which they picked up their forks and shook out their napkins. It was like a sneeze or a hiccup at the beginning of every meal.

This was not Miss Blue's style at all.

My very first breakfast at Charles, I had dumbly wandered across Dombey and Son to her table. This was her morning grace, spoken very slowly and with tears just beginning at the corners of her eyes:

Jesus, we hear you. We can hear you, dear Jesus. Your footsteps are coming closer. We know you are there. You can count on us. Dear Christ, appear before us in all your glory. Glory. We are your servants. We gather to thank you for our blessings. Dear Christ, do not be afraid we will betray you another time. You may approach. Receive our blessings for this food. Thank you and Amen.

(Cardmaker said with His luck He was probably the type who didn't like a lot of talking first thing in the morning.)

This second night of my life in Charles School, when the buzzer sounded signifying the students could be seated, we inched forward.

Cute Dibblee said, "There's too big a rush on Miss Horton's table, O torn cheeks; we might not all get to sit together if we aim for her."

"I'll chance it, thorn-brain," I said. "She seems to be the only normal person on the faculty and weirdos turn my stomach."

"You're surrounded by weirdos, O fingers-nailed," said Cardmaker. "Maybe you can arrange to be served in your room like Billy is."

We kept on that way, thinking up new ways to take off on O Bleeding Face, laughing and wisecracking our way into the dining room and across to Miss Horton's table.

She was in her twenties; she was this blonde who was only a few years out of the University of North Carolina where she'd belonged to Chi Omega sorority, and Cardmaker said that last year she'd tried to work through a petition that faculty could wear pants suits to teach in, but APE vetoed the idea with a raging lecture on Maturity. She spent a lot of time in The Caravan and smelled of cigarettes, and sometimes on an evening of gin, too. She probably enjoyed a martini or two before she had to face the *dum solas*. That was one of Cadet Butler Peabody's descriptions of us. It was a legal term, from the Latin *dum sola et casta*—translated: while single and chaste. Cardmaker told me he often wrote it in his letters to her. "That's all he knows about Charles School girls," she said.

Miss Horton had a boyfriend named John Bob White, who was up North somewhere studying to be a doctor. She talked a lot about this John Bob; it was a Southern thing, to call a person by two first names.

I was glad I didn't have to say much, because I was hungry, and because I'd begun to feel a little guilty at the tack our conversation had been taking in the queue. I didn't even let myself glance in the direction of Miss Blue's table. I was afraid everyone would still be sitting there with head bowed while the rest of us wolfed down hash and greens and corn muffins.

Cute Dibblee was doing a lot of talking, too. She was from the hills of West Virginia, and when she talked she said things like, "Well, it don't rain every time the pig squeals," and "The rooster makes more racket than the hen what laid the egg," and "A tater vine grows while you sleep."

Cardmaker said Cute was a Number Two, On The Ladder.

I liked listening to her and I liked her face. She was round-cheeked and large-eyed, with a pink complexion and a blonde Dutchboy haircut, and she smiled a lot. She looked like a Campbell's Soup kid, and she had a real Southern drawl.

Cardmaker said she was a poor white not too long before she came to Charles; her father had unexpectedly and suddenly come into a barrel of money with some invention of his for coal mines.

"Wait until you meet *him*!" Cardmaker had said.

"What about him?"

"Blood will tell."

"I still don't know what you mean."

"I mean you can take the man out of the hills, but you can't take the hills out of the man. You'll see. He loves to show up and take a batch of us down to the Stonewall Jackson Hotel for dinner."

I didn't pursue the subject. I was wondering how Cardmaker would judge my father. Never mind my *mother*! I didn't talk much about family.

Cardmaker said, "His name is Lorimer. Lorimer Will Dibblee. It's printed in gold on the side of his Lincoln Continental." She passed me the plate of corn muffins. "And Cute isn't a nickname either. She's got a sister called Sweet."

I felt a rush of loneliness, the type that comes for a second or two like great punches in the stomach and then goes without doing any damage, except to keep you ever alert to the idea that your life has changed completely, overnight. I was surrounded by strangers. Would

I ever really care about any of them? It didn't seem that way. I just felt numb and trapped and envious of Cardmaker, who was so wrapped up in everything and everyone.

For some sadistic reason Mail Queue came immediately after dinner every night except Sunday. I said "sadistic" because if you were really hungry and felt like a third helping of anything, and everyone else was through, they all stared at you with hatred while you finished. No one could leave a table until everyone there was through, no matter how eager a majority might be to get their mail.

Cardmaker said that APE had plotted it that way, so no one would eat a lot of dinner, because dinner was the most expensive meal.

It was Miss Horton who held up the table that night. She was dawdling over a second cup of coffee. "No one's going to get any mail," she said. "It's much too early. You've hardly been gone a day."

There were a few grumbles but we sat it out. I glanced across at APE's table, and noticed that Billy's feet didn't touch the floor. Then I watched Miss Mitchell, the gym teacher, smiling and winking across at Miss Able, the music teacher. Cardmaker said that if you noticed the musical selections Miss Able chose for chapel, you could pick out the message she was giving Miss Mitchell. "Thou Hast My Heart" was a favorite; Cardmaker said it was probably their song. ("Thou hast my heart, thou hast my heart, O Lord, how can I leave thee—")

As I was sitting there looking around, Miss Blue's table filed by. I saw her behind the girls, trying to see someone in the dining room to connect her eyes with in a greeting, an acknowledgment, something! She wore this sort of dazed half-smile, one hand clutching the silver cross. Why couldn't she leave the dining room with her eyes down, like APE? Why couldn't she realize that no one was going to call out, "Hi there, Miss Blue," or even smile or even nod? They just weren't, not for Miss Blue. For Miss Horton, maybe, for a few others, but not for Miss Blue.

I saw her see me and I glanced away. Then I wondered why I was being so small. Just as I was planning to glance back up and grin at her, Cardmaker said, "Here comes O gardenia smell divine. Look at her face! She looks like she shoots up!"

I didn't glance up at her or grin; I couldn't look at her face. I knew that look of expectancy. I also knew I hadn't made things any easier by telling everyone about the picture in the john.

"Dismissed," said Miss Horton.

We scrambled out of Dombey and Son Dining, I running past Miss Blue as though Mail Queue meant something to me. I wouldn't be hearing from my father for at least a week. . . . I'd asked my mother to stay out of my life. Completely.

Cardmaker received this letter from Butler Peabody.

Attention: Ms. Carolyn T. Cardmaker.
Re: Forthcoming Charles School Formal Dance.
Whereas we agreed to mutually partake of the social functions offered at our individual institutions, I shall be delighted to accept your invitation.

35

Whereas we agreed in special circumstances to attempt to provide a similar arrangement for a recommended party, I will provide one Ms. Flanders Brown with Cadet Sumner Thomas.

Be advised: Sumner Thomas of Baltimore, Maryland, is a fifteen-year-old, five-foot-seven-and-a half aspirant poet.

Whereas aforesaid Ms. Cardmaker did not advise this party of gown color, flowers will be red rose corsages for both Cardmaker and Brown, unless notification is received in 29 hours.

C.B.P. (Delivered by Hand)

"Listen, Cardmaker," I said, "I never asked you to do that!"

"I know that, but I got permission to telephone Butler last night, anyway."

"I don't want to be fixed up!"

"It's best at these particular welcoming functions, believe me."

"No!" I said. "Get me out of it!"

"Flanders," said Cardmaker, "all the other new girls are freshmen. You are a sophomore. Do you realize you'll be the only sophomore without a date if you don't accept Cadet Sumner Thomas? You'll be over in the bullpen with all the freshmen."

I hadn't thought of that.

CLANG—DONG DONG summoned us to evening study hall.

"You can thank me later," Cardmaker said, "and you will. Even if Sumner Thomas is bowlegged and walleyed. Anything's better than the bullpen."

That night after light bell, I stared out the window for a long time. I watched the stars and I watched the teachers going in and out of The Caravan, and I watched APE and Billy's lights.

I thought of my mother. I kept hearing her voice saying something over and over again, something that didn't have anything to do with anything going on in my life right then, but something she used to say a lot at mealtime. She was born up in Pennsylvania Dutch country, and sometimes she'd use one of the Pennsylvania Dutch expressions, as my grandmother used to do.

I just sat there on my bed in the dark, looking out the window and hearing her voice in my mind saying, "Eat what you can, what you can't eat we'll can."

I didn't cry, but I ached in my heart badly. Not for her. Never for her. But for life before Bobby Santanni, for family life, for sitting around a table eating dinner together, or coming home to them or having them come home, all the things you take for granted before you land in a place ruled by bells and strangers.

Then it went—it always goes, I've learned—and I felt okay but tired . . . and relaxed, strangely, as though I realized I was going to make it. I was going to get past things in this life, no matter what. I was going to be all right.

My eyes were closed. I was beginning to drift off, to start to sleep, when suddenly I heard it.

It was a wailing unlike any I had ever heard, not human, it couldn't be. A ghost? I didn't know. I froze. I listened. I heard it again and again.

If I'd been able to think clearly, I would have realized one thing about myself I'd never known before that moment: Whatever I would die of in this life, it would not be fright. If fright could have done it, I would have been dead already.

But I *was* as good as dead. Because when my door opened, I was paralyzed.

Five

"Dear?...Agnes is here."

It was Miss Blue's voice I heard as I lay there paralyzed. Then the overhead light in my small room was snapped on.

I was no longer powerless; I sat up in bed, rubbing my eyes against the light.

Miss Blue was not wearing her cross. She had on an old light blue wool bathrobe covering a long pink nightie. For the first time I realized that she did not have short gray hair at all. She'd been wearing it pinned back in a bun, but now it fell past her shoulders and she looked somewhat younger.

"I'm sorry, dear," she said, "but Agnes has just arrived from Birmingham, and I thought it would be nice if you became acquainted before morning."

"What was that terrible wailing in the hall just a second ago?" I said.

"There's something you should know about Agnes."

"Did she make that noise?"

"Dear, Agnes is a very pretty young lady whose father is a doctor, a prominent surgeon known worldwide, and Agnes is deaf and dumb."

It took me a while to sort out what she was telling me, and that she was not really telling me about a famous surgeon. She was telling me about the person I was to live with on Little Dorrit.

It still did not completely register.

Then Miss Blue stepped back and gave my door a tiny push with her bedroom slipper, and there stood this girl.

"This is Agnes Thatcher, dear." Miss Blue turned her back to me and said in a very slow and precise voice, and also loudly, "Agnes, this is Flanders Brown."

Before I tell you what Agnes Thatcher said, let me tell you what she looked like.

She was short—not as short as Billy, or even Cardmaker, but short and very slender, with shoulder-length hair so white-gold that at first I thought it wasn't real. Miss Blue was wrong—she wasn't pretty. To say that Agnes Thatcher was pretty was to say that the Grand Canyon was a hole, for Agnes was almost perfect, beautiful, the sort you turned to look at in a crowd and singled out to watch somewhere in a sea of faces, at a football game or concert, just to stare at. Her eyes were light green, there was some summer tan left on her clear, soft-looking skin, and her wide, full lips were smiling. She seemed like some enchanted angel.

She said—she *wailed*, "OWWWWL!" She seemed to lunge forward at me as she made this sound, with her mouth forming a large O.

"That means hello," said Miss Blue, noticeably rattled by the sound herself.

"Hi!" I said, speaking very loudly, too, and making an exaggerated hi with my mouth.

She said, "Lo Leet you."

"Pleased to meet you. That means pleased to meet you," said Miss Blue.

Again I worked my lips laboriously, answering, "Same here," and speaking in a loud voice.

Then Agnes said, "Gite."

I frowned when Miss Blue failed to translate for me, and I saw Miss Blue frowning, too.

"What?" I made my mouth say, my voice shout.

This time she barked the word at me, leaning closer to my face as though she was going to spit in my eye. "GITE!"

I just sat there, looking away from her, smoothing the ribbon along my blanket's edge.

Miss Blue said, "Well, now that you've met . . ." and her voice trailed off.

I whispered, "I don't know what she wants, or what gite means."

"It's all right, dear. You're both acquainted," said Miss Blue.

The next thing, Agnes Thatcher stamped her feet and shook her head and tried to say more forcibly the sound "gite," but it became a long, wailing, "GIIIIIIIIIIIIII-IIIITE!"

Her eyes were narrowed and she was showing great

irritation with both of us for not understanding. She was also carefully watching our lips. It would do no good for me to whisper, and I needn't have stretched my mouth all out of proportion, for she obviously was an excellent lip-reader.

I looked at her and shrugged my shoulders, smiling a little. "I just don't get it," I said.

She didn't smile back. She gave a heavy sigh and shook her head angrily.

"Well, I'm glad you're both acquainted." Miss Blue kept harping on the notion of our acquaintance, as though the mere fact of our meeting had been the primary obstacle to overcome.

Miss Blue said, "I think we'd better say good night."

At this, Agnes Thatcher grabbed her arm, gave it a punch, put one finger up in the air, and shook her head up and down in a "yes" gesture.

Then she said again, "Gite."

Still we didn't get it.

"We have to say good night, dear," Miss Blue told her.

She shook her head harder, shook her finger at Miss Blue, and repeated, "Gite!"

"Good night," I said, "is that it?"

She came dancing across to my bed with a big grin, and then, leaning down, she socked me in the shoulder. "Gite," she said.

I laughed, even though she hit hard and it hurt.

"Good night, Agnes."

"Gite."

"See you tomorrow."

"Lo leet you."

42

"Right," I said.

"Gite." She was backing out of the room with Miss Blue following.

I gave a little two-fingered salute with my hand. "So long."

As she disappeared from view, Miss Blue's hand still remained in my room, and I heard her shout, "Just a moment, Agnes. I'll come to tuck you in."

Her face and part of her body reappeared in my room.

"Isn't that sad, dear?" she said. "Jesus allows our afflictions to test us, but we sometimes forget 'His will be done' when we see the stricken."

"Is she next door to me?" I said. I knew she was. I could already hear her slamming things around in there, but I didn't want to go on talking with Miss Blue in that vein, about "the stricken" and "His will be done." I didn't take to the idea of God or Jesus treating whoever He felt like treating the same way a vivisectionist might treat a stray dog, testing someone's faith the way the dog might be tested for the physical side effects of a new drug.

"She's in 8, yes, dear. The sad thing is that she has an older sister, just as beautiful, and just like her. Dr. Thatcher sent her to a special school for the deaf, and she met another stricken as she was and married him. The doctor wants more for poor Agnes. He doesn't want her just to know the world of the handicapped. That's why he's doing differently with Agnes. A fine boarding school with high standards and a good reputation, then on to Sweet Briar for college. No special privileges to be granted to her, either. She's to participate in whatever the others participate in, be judged as they're judged. It's very brave of him, isn't it, Flanders?"

I said, "Of *him*?"

"Oh, she's brave, too, I'm sure. She seems brave."

"Gite," I moaned sarcastically.

But Miss Blue mistook my meaning. Her eyes brightened. "Yes," she bubbled. "She's stubborn. The way she insisted we understand what she wanted to say, what *gite* meant!"

I could hear hangers falling on the closet floor next door, and suitcases thumping against the walls. Since she could not hear herself, I doubted that she would be the quietest neighbor.

"I'll go to her now," said Miss Blue. "Good night, dear."

I sat there for a long while in the darkness, staring out at the night, listening to the sounds from the other room, and noticing the reflection of her light on the ivy outside my windowsill.

Gradually I made myself become oblivious to the chunking of baggage against walls, the slamming of drawers, and the wailing interspersed with Miss Blue's shouts. They were background noises like the sounds of workers putting up a house next to yours. I thought of other things, verses I had memorized, dates: dull insignificant things, the same way my father made long, detailed lists of things to do around the house, after my mother split—to keep his mind very busy but not with real thoughts.

Then the noises stopped; the lights went out.

I sank down under the covers and listened to some crickets.

About five minutes later I heard what sounded like an angry elephant charging, followed by a sound like air seeping from the tire of a huge trailer truck . . . angry elephant, air seeping, angry elephant, air seeping.

Of course. Agnes Thatcher snored.

Six

The first CLANG—DONG DONG of the day sounded at a quarter to seven. You had until seven thirty to dress and get yourself down to Dombey and Son for breakfast. After a nearly sleepless night, thanks to Agnes Thatcher's snoring, I fell back asleep until seven ten. Then I jerked awake, flew into my clothes, used the bathroom, and ran all the way down to the queue. There had been no sign of Agnes on Little Dorrit. Was she awake; how did she wake herself up in the morning? As the faculty line started to move past the queue, I wondered if it was my responsibility to go back and check on her.

I needn't have concerned myself, for in the next moment, Miss Blue appeared, marching in step with Agnes Thatcher, periodically doing a fast shuffle with her feet to stay in step. Miss Blue was also holding her right palm under but not quite touching Agnes' left elbow, as though she were escorting an elderly lady across the ice and was ready should she fall.

Agnes had no particular expression on her face; it was as ordinary as her face was extraordinary, perhaps slightly on the exasperated side where Miss Blue was concerned. Agnes seemed to want to walk ahead of Miss Blue, as though to deny they were a pair en route to breakfast. Miss Blue's expression was a little stranger than usual. There was the usual flush to her face, but the chin was thrust forward in a combative attitude, and there was a certain borrowed agony in her eyes, as though she was undertaking some of what she imagined to be Agnes' burden simply by walking alongside her.

Agnes did not join the queue, but continued along with Miss Blue into the dining room.

I was at the tail end of the queue. Cardmaker and Cute were far ahead of me. When I got inside Dombey and Son, I hurried to get the last chair at Miss Balfour's table. I didn't have to look back toward Miss Blue's to know that Agnes would be there with her.

Miss Balfour was the school dietician. Cardmaker liked to describe people by saying things like: "For Sue Crockett, hell will be a place where no one knows her mother drives a Mercedes," or "For Ditty Hutt, heaven will be a place where you can marry your own brother." The other night, after Miss Balfour oversaw the first study hall of the year, Cardmaker had remarked, "For Miss Balfour, hell will be a place with no mirrors." Miss Balfour had spent most of the hour and a half peeking at herself in the mirror of her compact. Cardmaker said she belonged to a club called "The World of Beauty," and every two months received a huge package containing cosmetic samples. "She's had her face lifted twice," Cardmaker told me, "and she's supposed to be way over sixty."

She looked around forty. She was a skinny woman who probably wouldn't fare well at all in a strong wind. She had very black hair, big round blue eyes made up with mascara and eyeliner, and dabs of rouge on her cheeks like a department-store doll.

Grace at Miss Balfour's table was simple to the point of being almost nonexistent. She snapped her napkin to her lap with a flourish and her head bowed, while rattling off "Thank thee for this food." Then she poured the coffee from the pot with one hand while the other delivered it to her lips, and after this snappy maneuver, her eyes went directly to the large mirror on the opposite wall. She sipped her coffee (she ate no breakfast) and watched her own expressions and poses.

Behind me I could hear Miss Horton holding forth on John Bob, and I could see Billy, down at APE's table, carefully spreading apple butter on johnnycake, his little feet dangling above the floor.

I had never eaten fried apples with bacon before, and I was going at it tentatively, mulling over whether or not it was fair to call this breakfast. At the table, everyone except Miss Balfour and me was a senior. After I introduced myself, I was ignored. They were all busy discussing the dance, which was then two days away.

I was for no good reason threatening myself with another awful daydream. In this one my date for the dance was a divine number who was being made to pay off some enormous penalty by escorting me. I'd been doing that sort of thing to myself a lot since my mother had left; I'd also been having a lot of little accidents. My father had discussed the accidents with me, asking me if I thought I was acting out the feeling of rejection.

"Not that I know of," I'd answer him.

"Are you sure, honey? Because you know Mom didn't really reject you. She simply felt she had to find herself. She felt *she* was being rejected."

"She was just horny for Bobby," I said.

"There's more to it than that, Flan."

"I don't care if she did reject me. I reject her back," I said.

"She loves you very much, Flan."

"I noticed," I said.

When I came to the point in my daydream when my date was eyeing the stag line, trying to get someone's, *anyone's*, eye, to see if he could unload me on him, I heard someone say, "Little Dorrit."

I looked up.

"I said don't *you* live on Little Dorrit?"

I knew her name and that she was the most everything of the senior class. Cardmaker had told me that about every other year or so there's a most everything in the senior class: most beautiful, most brilliant, most poised, most sexy, most talented and most you name it. Cardmaker said that so far in our class there was no candidate for most everything, but a lot of the best girls didn't arrive until junior year.

The girl speaking to me was France Shipp. She'd been born on Bastille Day, which was how she got the neat first name; how she got all the rest, the dark red hair and fabulous figure and great face and 140 I.Q. and everything, I can't answer: Fate, God, Good Genes, I don't know.

She was also engaged, the only senior who was engaged, with a genuine two-carat diamond. Her fiancé was the son of a senator and a freshman at Yale. Whenever he couldn't attend the Charles School dances, France Shipp became a "Junior Chaperone," which was the same thing as a faculty chaperone: She watched over the dance.

"Yes, I live on Little Dorrit," I told her. "I have slight asthma." I added that so she would not imagine worse things—that the full moon grew hair all over my body and made my teeth into fangs, or that I wandered the school halls nights with a carving knife.

"Agnes Thatcher arrived, didn't she?"

"Yes. She rooms next door to me."

France then explained to everyone that Agnes was deaf and dumb.

"Her sister's also deaf and dumb, but what a doll!" France said. "I met her husband, who's deaf and dumb, too, at our cup race last summer. Her husband is a fabulous racer. He won the Miami–Montego Bay Silver Pineapple one year."

"He must be rich," another senior said.

"Filthy!" France laughed.

I didn't have to ask Cardmaker their numbers. They were both Twos, On the Ladder. I was beginning to tell a Two by her conversation.

"Does *your* father still race, France?"

"Not ocean racing any longer. We sold *Thetis*," France said. She was no longer including me in the conversation, or bothering to look in my direction. "Incidentally," she said, "Agnes Thatcher would be a perfect bet for E.L.A."

E.L.A. was *the* secret society at Charles School. (It was also the only one allowed.) No one but members knew what the initials stood for. All the members got special privileges; they even had a room of their own where no one else could go. They were the honored keepers of the library and could study in the library instead of under the supervision of faculty in study hall. Cardmaker called them the Extra Lucky Asses.

"We're past due to pledge someone with a handicap," Loretta Dow spoke up. She was the president of E.L.A. She had rust-colored hair, a space between her front teeth, and the largest wardrobe of anyone at Charles. Cardmaker said she never repeated an outfit over a month's time. She also went to Richmond overnight every Wednesday to see a shrink.

"The father is Win Thatcher," said France Shipp. "My mother says he has so much money it's gross. Not from being a doctor. Inherited. And Mrs. Thatcher is a Lovecraft."

"Is Agnes a freshman?" Loretta Dow asked.

France Shipp deigned to look in my direction. "Flanders?"

"I don't know," I said. "I just met her last night."

"Perhaps we ought to find out if Peter Rider could be talked into being her escort Saturday night at the dance?"

"We haven't even laid eyes on her," another senior said, also E.L.A.

"Maybe Peter wouldn't want to be pawned off on her," another.

"Peter would be happy to help out if he's free," France said. Then, "Flanders? Which one is she?"

I turned around and looked back at Miss Blue's table. "She's the blonde on Miss Blue's right."

France and the others looked.

France said, "Mon Dieu! I would say that Peter Rider would be très très interested."

"Why would he?" said another. "He can't see."

"He likes to be with beautiful girls just the same," said France. "Peter says they give off the best vibrations."

"I think Peter Rider is sex-eeeeeee!" said one of the seniors. "He can try out his Braille on my bod anytime!"

"I'll drink to that," said another, raising her glass of milk in a toast.

"That turns me on just to think about," one said.

Miss Balfour's eyes suddenly came into a half-focus. "All you think about is boys," she said. But it was as though she was talking to herself, because she was looking directly at her own reflection.

After breakfast there was an hour before morning assembly at nine. When I left Dombey and Son, I went directly to Hard Times, to see if I could find Cardmaker. I wanted to complain bitterly about the seniors, and the way they talked about Agnes making a good bet for E.L.A., and fixing up Agnes for the dance, without caring anything about me.

I found Cardmaker in the Hard Times john, bent over the bathtub. The tub was swimming with navy blue water, and there was something soaking in it.

"I'm dyeing my formal again," Cardmaker said. "I dyed it last year, too. It was white when I wore it in our church Christmas pageant. I was Mary. It was pale green last year. . . . How do you like her? I saw her at breakfast."

"I don't know yet, but the seniors are already talking about making her an E.L.A."

I told Cardmaker the whole story while she swished the gown around in the navy blue water.

"That's just like them to lump together the blind and the deaf," Cardmaker said. "This is a net gown and it's practically in pieces from these dye jobs and from my putting my foot through the skirt. Does she use sign language?"

"I haven't seen her use it yet," I said. I explained about *owl* and *lo leet you* and *gite*.

"She isn't dumb if she talks," Cardmaker said.

"It's not really talking."

"Dumb means mute. She's not mute."

"She's rich," I said.

"I guessed that. If the Extra Lucky Asses want her, she'd have to be. They'd never take a Four who wasn't."

"Loretta Dow said they were past due to pledge someone with a handicap," I said.

Cardmaker snickered. "She doesn't see the space between her own front teeth as a handicap?" Cardmaker wiped her hands off on her slip, leaving dye prints down the side. "Miss Blue was walking around with Agnes Thatcher at breakfast as though she'd won her knocking over bottles with a ball at a carnival."

I had to get back to Little Dorrit to make my bed and clean my room before the next CLANG—DONG DONG.

When I got there, I saw Agnes standing in the doorway of the bathroom. I smiled and waved, and noticed she was carrying a picture and some Scotch tape.

She beckoned me to her with her finger and then indicated that I should step inside. She pointed at the picture of Jesus, and clamped her nose with her finger.

I said, "It's not mine. It's Miss Blue's."

She stuck out her tongue and shook her head back and forth.

I said, "I'm not crazy about it, either. It's depressing."

She frowned.

"De-*pressing*!" I said.

Agnes nodded. Then she held up a finger for attention.

She walked across to the wall, and beside the picture of Christ's head she placed the picture she was carrying. It looked like it had been torn from a book. She Scotch-taped it to the wall.

When she was done, she turned and nodded positively, smiling.

It was a photograph of a man with a beard, a head-and-shoulders shot.

I said, "Who is it?"

"Dee Day Door Den." She managed the sounds with considerable effort.

I said, "I'm sorry, Agnes. I don't understand you."

That same look of impatience came across her face that I had seen there last night.

"DEEDAYDOORDEN!" She said it fast and loud.

I said, "I'm *sorry*."

She made some disgruntled sound and sighed and went across the hall to her room. I was going to follow, and then I couldn't see what good it would do if I did.

For what? To apologize because I couldn't translate her noises into words? Why did she get so angry because I couldn't? Why was she so impatient?

I went into my room and began throwing my bed together, realizing that I was a little irritated myself. Why *me*? Why *me* with Miss Blue to contend with and now Agnes Thatcher?

I was bending over to tuck in my sheets when I felt this punch in my ribs.

I let out a yelp of pain, stood up, and faced Agnes.

"Don't punch me!" I said. "It hurts!"

She ignored this and thrust a piece of paper at me.

She had written across it: "D.H. Lawrence is my favorite writer."

I looked down at her and tried to force a smile, even though my ribs still stung from her punch. I said, "That's neat, Agnes."

She nodded and pointed back toward the bathroom.

Then she made those noises again. "Dee Day Door Den."

Seven

On the Saturday night of the big dance, after dinner, I was standing in Mail Queue when Cute Dibblee tapped me on the shoulder.

"Flanders, you want to have dinner with my pappy and me and Cardmaker after church tomorrow?"

"Sure," I said. "When did your father come to Wales?"

"He'll be here tonight. He's bringing a cousin of mine to be my date for the dance."

"Neat!"

"Would *you* want to go with *your* cousin?"

"I guess not," I said.

"Pappy always brings some relative to be my date. He don't trust other boys," she said. "We'll all go out to the Stonewall Jackson for Sunday dinner."

"Thanks, Cute."

"Get permission from your faculty chum tonight," she said.

There was actually mail in my box, my first letter from my father, and a letter from Carol MacLean who lived next door to us when we were in Rochester, New York.

I read my father's letter immediately.

Dear Flan-Tan,
So far we have sixty seekers enrolled and we are planning marathon sessions for the first weekend they are in residence. I think there is a good chance of my being interviewed on Controversy. If so, they'll be moving in with their cameras in a week to ten days.

I don't think you should plan a visit until sometime in late October. I'm disappointed, too, Flan, but there just isn't time to get everything done properly.

I paused long enough to remember Cardmaker's statement that most Number Threes were more Number Three than they thought they were.

Your mother has written several times asking about you. While I am not legally obligated to give her any information concerning your whereabouts, I wish you would reconsider. I am the last person to sing your mother's praises at this point; still, I think it is wrong for you to cut her out of your life.

She is living in New York City at 58 West 9th Street. You might drop her a line.

Flanny, I miss you so. Don't get too lonely and mistake seductive rituals for solutions to life's prob-

lems. Prayer is only talking to yourself. It's good to do that. But don't be fooled into thinking some higher power hears you . . . much less cares a damn about what you have to say. In this life, Flan, it's all up to you. With a little help from your friends, as the Beatles would say.

   Write often, honey.

*Love,
Dad*

I decided to open Carol's letter in my room. I wasn't ready for more flak. My mother had waited until we'd moved from Auburn to run off with Bobby, but by then word must have drifted back.

My father's letter had put me in a mood for anything but a dance. I understood that he was busy—it wasn't that. It was the fact he'd actually written out my mother's address that way. I didn't want her address or any proof at all that she existed.

I really don't think I would have minded so much if it had been my father who had run off with someone younger. I might have hated it because he was my favorite parent and I would have missed him, but it wouldn't have been shameful or humiliating, I don't think. Men did that sort of thing all the time.

What made me really furious at her was that it just wasn't like her. She wasn't this original thinker, this big Individual. She was just an ordinary woman, except for a few bright ideas she'd picked up from my father. I could remember hearing my father say something at the dinner table one night, and a few weeks later hearing my mother mouth it word-for-word when she was talking with my Aunt Helen.

Sometimes when she helped my father out with his various projects she tried to learn everything she could about the subject, but mostly she just took up time with dumb questions and impossible suggestions.

If she'd been this great free spirit, this troubled intellect, I could easily explain her skipping off the way she did; but to my way of thinking it was exactly the way it appeared to be: middle-aged woman gets the hots for young boy.

I just hoped that when he dumped her, she didn't show up on our doorstep. My next thought struck me with a large stab of loneliness: I didn't even know what "our doorstep" looked like; when I thought of going home, I couldn't even picture home. I'd never been there.

I was walking down Little Dorrit when I heard Miss Blue call out, "Dear? We're having a little chum chat."

Agnes Thatcher was standing just outside the bathroom, wearing a long red silk robe with a gold dragon on the back. When she saw me she made a face, the sort one makes to commiserate with another when both are sharing the same sorry fate.

"I know you girls are anxious to get ready for the dance," Miss Blue said, "and I'm not going to take a lot of your time." She was shouting again, making her lips form each syllable. She walked into the bathroom, beckoning at us to follow.

"The wall," she said with a flourish of her hand as she waved it toward the two pictures next to the mirror, "is not a photograph gallery. When I acknowledged His presence with a small token, I was not suggesting that we all start a pinup collection."

Miss Blue was addressing me, not Agnes, though the shouting and facial contortions were for Agnes' benefit. It was clear that Miss Blue believed I was the culprit.

"Just who is this positioned next to our Lord Jesus, Flanders?"

"It's D.H. Lawrence, Miss Blue."

"Are you intending a joke of some sort? Because it's in very bad taste."

At this point Agnes thumped her chest like Tarzan and pointed to the picture, then thumped her chest again.

"You did this, Agnes?"

Agnes nodded yes.

"But *why*?"

Agnes' mouth opened to answer but Miss Blue held up a finger to silence her. "No," she said, "never mind. You can write me a note about it. There isn't time now. The point is, Agnes, it has to come down!"

Agnes shook her head no.

"It *does*, dear. We can't just paste up anything we want on the walls." Miss Blue was shouting again.

When I left them, Agnes was still firmly shaking her head no and Miss Blue's pink flush was spreading to a scarlet one.

On my bed there was a florist's box, which had been delivered by the porter during the dinner hour. Inside were the promised red roses and a card written in a sprawling hand.

It said, *DON'T EVER CHANGE. Sumner Thomas.*

How could someone who had never laid eyes on me tell me not to change?

There was probably something wrong with him mentally.

I began to feel really upset; my father's term for the feeling was "severe angst." I sat down on the bed and held my head with my hands. One of the Attitudes, Inc., exercises for anxiety was to stretch out with your feet raised above your head. Then you were to shut your eyes and remember a difficult period from which you thought you'd never recover. You were to try and think how you recovered and why. You were to ask youself how much credit you deserved for recovering. The idea was supposed to be that in reflection a person usually saw that he had come through things on his own power, and that often the things were less threatening than he had thought at the time.

I put my feet up on the headboard of the bed. I closed my eyes. (This could have nothing to do with my mother since she had never existed.)

The difficult period was when I had cheated on a composition for History. We were studying systems of government. I favored anarchy, like my father; I had copied a lot about anarchists from the encyclopedia. My teacher recognized the text; the school principal wrote my father a letter. Because he was out of town, I spent three wretched days waiting for him to deal with me. When he finally came home and read the letter, he came into my bedroom for a talk. He said I would be a lousy anarchist because obviously I was a follower. I had to copy other people's ideas and words. He said I was more fit for fascism, where someone ruled me totally, my thoughts, my actions, my prejudices, everything. He said in a democracy I'd be one of those who'd vote Republican because my family always had, that I'd never go out on my own and investigate the issues. He went on and on that way, bawling me out and at the same time giving me his own version of systems of government, which didn't always agree with my schoolbooks.

I couldn't see where *I* deserved any credit for recovering from that anxiety attack; my father deserved it all.

Somehow this made me all the more depressed, and I decided to make everything even worse by reading Carol MacLean's letter.

It was filled with gossip about people I would never see again. Then at the very end, there was this paragraph:

> *I know you must feel down about what your mother did, but in a way it was supercourageous. I mean, I hope when I am practically forty years old I still want to make out, enough to leave home and security, too! I don't even want to make out that badly now, and I am getting ancient, sixteen next month. Don't get me wrong, Flan, because I know it's not easy for you, but do you know what I mean? My mother is okay but she has no sex life (except my father), which is bound to be boring by now, so she doesn't have the nerve to do things that are original.*

I had been expecting her to make fun of my mother, or at least write that people were shocked. "Supercourageous" wasn't exactly what I had in mind for an adjective that would suit my mother.

I put the letter under my desk blotter and stared across at my formal, which was hanging on the back of my door. It was very simple, black, silk, sleeveless and backless, with a low-cut front. My father had helped me pick it out in New York at Lord & Taylor. It was the first formal I'd ever owned.

As soon as I was undressed, I realized I was going to look awful. There were two huge black-and-blue marks on my body, one on my shoulder and one lower near my rib cage. These were the results of Agnes Thatcher's demanding my attention with her punches.

I decided that I had been tolerant long enough . . . tolerant of the fact that her snoring kept me awake nights; that her normal way of closing a drawer or a closet door was to slam it shut so hard my walls shook; that her little jokes to herself early in the morning, or late at night, made all the monstrous rasping asthma attacks of my entire life, by comparison, seem to have occurred underneath thirty pillows.

I put on my robe and went out into the hall. The bathroom was empty. The picture of D.H. Lawrence was down. I knocked on Agnes' door long enough to realize she couldn't know I was doing it. I opened the door slowly and poked my head inside.

There was an open suitcase on the bed. Agnes was angrily tossing things into it: pajamas, toothbrush, toothpaste, slippers.

A white taffeta formal was spread out on the bed. Agnes was wearing jeans.

She felt my presence and turned around.

I said, "Are you mad because Miss Blue made you take down the picture?"

There was a notebook on the small desk beside her bed. Agnes wrote in it.

I just found out my date is blind!

"He's a blind date." I smiled. I was in a snide mood.

She made a fist and brought it up close to my face. She wrote: *Not funny! I am not going to look like a carny act, like the sideshow of the dance.*

"He's supposed to be very good-looking," I said. "You want my date instead? He wrote 'Don't ever change' on the card with the flowers, and he's never met me, doesn't know anything about me. He's probably backward."

Agnes made a gesture as though she were brushing away flies.

Anyway, she wrote, *I'm going to the infirmary. Miss Blue says anyone not at the dance must be in the infirmary.*

"Just because your date is blind?" I said.

We'd create a spectacle together!

"Have you told anyone you're not keeping the date with him?"

"Ma Boo," she said.

"What did Miss Blue say?"

She said she couldn't force me to go to the dance.

"France Shipp's going to be mad at you," I said.

This time when she held her nose with her fingers, she used the other hand to reach up high in the gesture of someone pulling a chain. Then she went back to packing.

I went away without showing her my black-and-blue marks. I took a shower and washed my hair. While it was drying I watched myself in the mirror the way Miss Balfour did.

Then I got my answers ready.

It was my father who taught me about having my answers ready. He told me that instead of dreading questions that might arise, situations, subject matters, et cetera, it was always good to anticipate as much as I could and have my answers ready.

I came up with two.

1. I'm not feeling suicidal tonight . . . in case I was offered a cigarette. Cardmaker said it happened all the time because the cadets could smoke. If we were caught at it, we'd be expelled.

2. I'm sorry but I have a bad hangover from last night . . . in case I was offered anything out of a flask, which Cardmaker said happened all the time, too.

There was supposed to be a 3, but I couldn't think of it. My experience where sex was concerned was zero. I'd known kids who'd made out by fourteen, and I hadn't even French kissed or done a damn thing below the waist. Since I was twelve, we'd never lived anyplace long enough for me to get very well acquainted with boys, and right after my mother ran off with Bobby, I went through a man-hating stage. I didn't care if I ever had sex.

I knew I was past that stage when Cardmaker showed me her pornography collection. It had been listed in the Senior Will as "Valuable Pictures" and left to her by a Hard Times resident who'd graduated. Cardmaker had never made it either, but she had done more things than I had, and she'd made up her mind to do everything by the time she graduated. She kept a checklist in the back of a book of Diane Wakoski poems.

According to Cardmaker you couldn't get away with much at a formal dance unless you were an E.L.A. member. (They had keys to a lot of the doors, but they were not supposed to be the types who wanted to get away with much; that was why their honor system worked.) All the action took place in stairwells and during dark numbers on the dance floor. If it was possible to position yourself near an area chaperoned by Miss Able and Miss Mitchell together (which sometimes happened) you could go fairly far, since they were too taken with each other to excel as lookouts.

The gym doors were locked so no one could go outside to the bushes.

By the time CLANG—DONG DONG announced that the dance was ready to begin, that the cadets from Wales were arriving, I was dressed and pinned with the corsage. I had covered my black-and-blue marks with makeup and sneaked on some faint eyeliner, although we were not supposed to wear anything but pancake, powder, light lipstick, and light mascara.

When I went into the bathroom to check my makeup in the bright light there, instead of seeing my reflection in the mirror, I saw a piece of notebook paper. It was as familiar as the writing across it.

TO ALL CONCERNED. NOTICE FROM YOURS TRULY.
"I worship Christ, I worship Jehovah, I worship Pan, I worship Aphrodite. But I do not worship hands nailed and running with blood upon a cross...."
D.H. Lawrence, 1912

Eight

Before I went down to the reception room to meet my date, I had to ask Miss Blue for permission to eat Sunday dinner with Cute Dibblee and her father. She was sitting in her favorite chair on David Copperfield, under the huge painting of Mary, Queen of Scots, at the top of the stairs.

"Don't you have a little black handkerchief, Flanders?" she asked me once she had consented to my Sunday outing. She was dressed in a black gown with a high neck and long sleeves, and she was wearing her cross.

"No one carries handkerchiefs anymore," I said. I noticed for the first time the printing on the plaque under the painting. It said: *DEATH-CELL PRAYER OF MARY, QUEEN OF SCOTS before she placed her head on the executioner's block. At the decree of her own cousin, also a woman.* There was more printing at the bottom of the painting itself, but it was too small for me to read.

"I wasn't thinking that you should *carry* a handkerchief," said Miss Blue. "You need one for the front of your dress. It's cut much too low."

"There's nothing there for anyone to see anyway," I said.

"It is not decent, Flanders. We'll fix it."

She loaned me a small square of black lace handkerchief and helped me pin it in place.

By the time I got down to the reception room, I had missed the march of W.M.A. boys as they came up the hill. It was supposed to be one of the highlights of the dance. I hated Miss Blue for meddling, first in Agnes' affairs, and then with the front of my gown. I stood beside Miss Balfour in Reception, waiting for my name to be called, and I complained about Miss Blue.

"All you girls think about is yourselves," she said. I thought that was a strange remark coming from someone who was most of the time mesmerized by a mirror. She was all in red for the dance, red shoes even. She looked like a little hand puppet, she was so small and her face was made up like a doll's, with circles of rouge and spit curls across her forehead. Her bright red lipstick made a distinct Cupid's bow.

She said, "You girls make everything sound worse than it is, telling rumors about things that are supposed to be in the food, for example."

"I don't tell rumors about the food at all," I said.

"You will if you hang around Carolyn Cardmaker

much longer," she said. "If you walk with ducks, you start waddling before long."

Then I heard my name.

Into the room stepped a young man in dark blue jodhpurs with shiny black boots and a light blue military-style jacket. There were gold epaulets on the shoulder.

"He's got boots and jodhpurs on. He's cavalry," said Miss Balfour. "Step forward."

I did, hoping I hadn't already begun to waddle.

"Cadet Sumner Thomas," a man's voice proclaimed.

We walked toward each other. As he came two steps from me, he stopped abruptly, and like the mechanical man performing, his arm shot out in a crook, ready for me to put my arm through it.

I did, vaguely aware that Cute Dibblee's name was being called next.

"For a blind date, you're okay," said Sumner Thomas in a surprised tone. He had a good face, gray eyes, a pug nose, and tight curly blond hair. He could have been taller, and thinner, but I thought he was okay, too.

"I haven't made up my mind yet about you," I said. "I hear you're in the cavalry."

"Didn't you see my entrance?"

"No."

"That's why you haven't made up your mind about me. You've never seen me on horseback."

"How come you made up your mind without seeing *me* on horseback?" I said.

"I like redheads, that's why. Do you want to hear my prospectus?"

"What's that?"

"Do you want to hear all about me?" he said as we were walking along Bleak House toward the gym.

"Okay, go ahead."

"Okay. Number one, my father has no money. He had to practically liquidate all his holdings to send me off to W.M.A. I wait on table for extra money, groom the academy horses, and M.C. some of the academy affairs. My mother's dead."

"Mine is, too," I said. "Sort of."

"Mine was this gorgeous bitch who killed herself."

"Mine isn't actually really dead. But she ran off with someone young enough to be her own son."

"Mine left a note you won't believe. You want to hear what she wrote?"

"Okay," I said.

"She wrote: 'Everyone is to blame for this. Everyone who reads this note or hears about it. Sincerely, Beddi Thomas.'"

"How awful!"

"So now you're to blame for her suicide, too, because you heard about it," he said. "Someday if I ever make a lot of money, I'm going to throw a huge party for everyone to blame for my mother's death. A lot of people have heard about her note, and most of them have told others. I could probably fill a hotel with all those responsible."

"Why did she feel that way?"

He shrugged. "She was a dramatic type. She'd wanted to be an actress really badly, and she sort of was one for a while. But my father finally made her give up her career."

"Did it happen a long time ago?"

"Last Christmas Eve," he said. "Her timing was dramatic, too."

"You're lucky you can talk about it so calmly," I said.

"I can talk about it; why shouldn't I talk about it?" he said.

"That's what I said," I said. "You're lucky you can talk about it."

"When did yours run off?" he said.

"At the end of summer."

"Mine was in the bottom of the bottle half the time."

"She was where?"

"She drank," he said.

"Mine didn't have that for an excuse."

"She loved the theater. Every fall she went up to New York and saw all the openings. She was in summer stock once, in Connecticut, doing Shakespeare."

"Mine never wanted to be anything but what she was until a certain Italian came on the scene."

"I never saw her stagger or get thick-tongued or sloppy," he said. "I never saw her in bad shape, no matter how much she drank."

"Mine got drunk once. She had to, to tell my father she was leaving."

"Mine was beautiful."

"Mine wasn't beautiful," I said.

"Jesus, it's morbid to talk about the dead at a dance."

"My father is a truly handsome man though."

"How'd we get started on all this parental crap? We ought to change the subject if you ask me."

We were approaching the entrance to the gym. Ahead of us I could see Billy, and the glimmer of light from his gold Phi Beta Kappa key. He was wearing a white carnation in the lapel of his dinner jacket.

"Did you see the clown behind me in line at Reception?" Sumner asked.

"No."

"He's not W.M.A. He's not in uniform at all, and he's not in a tux or a dinner jacket. He's this big farmer in white ducks and a blue jacket."

"Whose date is he?"

"I was going to ask you. We were all standing out front by the rose bushes, waiting for Reception to be started. There's fertilizer that's just been put down. This dumb oaf suddenly speaks up in this real hillbilly twang, and says 'Smells lak somebody farted.'"

I remembered then that the name after mine had been Cute Dibblee. Sumner was probably describing her cousin. I also remembered the card with the roses.

"What did your card mean?" I said.

"My mother taught me about it," he said. "It's an opening-night thing, and this is sort of our opening night. On opening night in theater it's bad luck to wish something good, so you send bad wishes, like 'Break a leg' or 'Fall down a flight of stairs.'"

"What does 'Don't ever change' have to do with bad wishes?"

"Think about it," he said.

"Yes," I said. "I think I get it now."

"Are we going to have the same agreement Cardmaker and Peabody have?"

"I don't know. Are we?"

"It's very practical. There are no strings."

"What if someone likes strings?" I said.

"Someone had better get it out of her head," he said.

"Well, it's the last thing I want. Strings," I said.

"It's out of the question," he said.

"*I* don't even want to discuss it," I said.

"It's for real mid-West, WASP, Republican straights," he said. "It's not for me."

"If I thought it was for you," I said, feeling more and more disappointed, "I'd split."

Then I decided to change the subject. "Butler said you're a poet."

"I am."

"Give me an original line or two."

"Here goes," he said.

"That's right I want everything about you including the body you are are hiding in. I'll take that first and then I'll rape your eyes."

"Oh," I said. "I see." I didn't. Not at all.

We were face to face with Billy. Behind him, inside the gym, I could see APE in a long, light blue dress with a lace front and a long rope of pearls swinging off her bosom.

I said, "Mr. Ettinger, I would like to present Cadet Thomas."

"*Dr.* Ettinger, please, Miss Brown."

"Cadet Thomas," I said, "this is Dr. Ettinger."

We were nicely performing all these little rituals when out of the corner of my eye I suddenly caught the glint of a diamond's sparkle, then another glitter. I looked and saw APE moving her diamond up and down, rubbing it. Cardmaker had warned me she only did that in rage.

Then she said my name and I knew she was angry.

"Come here! By yourself, Flanders!"

I placed my palm over the black lace handkerchief and inched forward.

"I want to know the meaning of all this, Flanders!"

"My father didn't think it was an indecent dress, Mrs. Ettinger."

"You may tell your father that it is clearly verging on indecency," she said, "but I'm interested more in the doings on Little Dorrit!"

"The practicing?"

"The pinning up of pictures and sayings in the bathroom. I'm just sick in bed about it!"

"I had nothing to do with it, Mrs. Ettinger."

"Then it was clearly your responsibility to report to me the destruction of school property."

"Yes, ma'am."

"I was astounded to go up on Little Dorrit a short while ago and discover that certain students have taken it upon themselves to blaspheme Jesus Christ by hanging his picture beside a bathroom mirror. I gather the D.H. Lawrence quotation is a comment upon the picture by a second student!"

"Miss Blue put Jesus up there," I said.

APE stopped what seemed to be a sputtering start of another harangue, this one on D.H. Lawrence. She stared down at me. "Miss Blue?"

"I don't think she intended blasphemy."

"Students, my dear Flanders, do not make a habit of thinking about what it is that may motivate a member of the faculty. You may return to your partner."

It was in the middle of the second Paul Jones of the evening that I felt the beginnings of the attack.

I needed air badly.

Miss Horton tried to help me by leading me out into the hall and unlocking the doors which opened onto the playing fields.

"You're not supposed to set foot out here during a dance unless you're an E.L.A. senior," she said, "and then only to allow your date a smoke. . . . But I think we can make an exception under the circumstances."

I was bent double coughing and wheezing.

I had left Sumner with Cardmaker and Cadet Peabody. Cardmaker's neck had turned blue; her perspiration had activated the dye she'd used on her formal. They were trying to figure out a solution.

Sumner had said, "Try to get a hold of yourself so you can come back, will you? Asthma is all psychological, anyway."

"Thanks," I said. "You're marvelously sensitive, tactful, and sympathetic."

The only other thing I'd really noticed at the dance, besides Cardmaker's blue neck, was the very tall, loose-boned boy in the white ducks and the blue coat—Cute Dibblee's cousin. He had rust-colored hair as silky looking as a prince's and real dimples with this big wide white smile. I thought as I looked at him that a girl could forgive someone with a face like that for saying just about anything, but probably my overworked bronchi were taxing my brain.

"It's a beautiful night, isn't it?" Miss Horton said as I struggled for breath.

I turned away from her to try to expire the deep breath of air I'd inhaled. Suddenly I saw them. They were way over near the bleachers, spotlighted by a circle of moonlight. She was the most everything in a white net formal as well as in any old thing at the breakfast table in Dombey and Son. He was a W.M.A. most everything, judging from all the paraphernalia attached to the front of his jacket, ribbons and circles of gold and badges.

They were just about to kiss. She reached up and removed his dark glasses.

"Do you feel any better, Flanders?" Miss Horton asked me.

Even though I was gasping for breath, and trying frantically to convey to Miss Horton the knowledge that I did not feel better, the old mind was clicking.

Dark glasses . . . dark glasses at night.

France Shipp had used her E.L.A. privilege to slip away from her Junior Chaperone duties to be with Peter Rider. Peter Rider was not interested in a smoke, either, from what I'd observed.

That was my last clear thought before I found myself on Great Expectations, in the nurse's examining room of the infirmary.

After the injection of epinephrine the nurse told me I was to stay in the infirmary sleeping room all night.

"Why not my own room on Little Dorrit?"

"On the evening of a dance, one must either attend the dance or stay in the infirmary."

She said she would send for Miss Blue and have my pajamas brought to me. I went into the sleeping room to wait for them.

"Owl!" I heard. "Owl!"

It was dark. I could just make out her silhouette near the window. I walked across to her and stood in the moonlight so she could see my lips.

"I had an asthma attack."

She ignored this information and pointed out the window. She had a view of the playing fields, the bleachers, and France Shipp with Peter Rider.

"He's handsome," I said. "He could have been your date."

She didn't respond to my remark. Instead she moaned, "Dexxxxxxxxxx," howled and giggled, hunching her shoulders and making this bizarre face with all her teeth showing in a grimace.

"Dex!" she cackled. "Dex!"

She turned her back to me and stared out the window, the huge gold dragon on the back of her robe facing me menacingly.

I tapped her on the shoulder. "Just the preliminaries, Agnes," I said. "Not the real thing."

She gave me one of her famous mean and hard punches. Her face was cross. She looked around until she saw the pencil she had left on one of the infirmary cots, the pad beside it.

She scribbled: *I know about sex!*

"Good," I said. "Now try to learn how to get someone's attention without boxing them."

"Gite!" she said. She turned her back on me again and went to the window to look out.

The epinephrine worked so well I was able to sleep through Agnes' snoring.

Before I closed my eyes I thought I had the answer to the suddenness of my asthma attack. Sumner Thomas had come to Charles School on horseback. He had also announced that he groomed the academy horses. Animal dander was enough to trigger one off. I fell asleep believing that had to be the reason.

When I woke up it was early morning. The sun was streaming in through the open window, and there was a strong breeze. Agnes was asleep under the covers, but her writing material was scattered about the room. I recovered most of it, including the second page of a letter, left unfinished.

2.

said she met you and Don one summer at a race. It was her idea to fix me up with this blind guy. She said if she didn't have a guy herself, she'd fall for him. I was all set to go but then I just couldn't. It wasn't that he was blind. It was my same old fear of boys. Who would want me? I can never act like everyone else because I'm not like everyone else, and this is not going to work. Tell Dad that I want to come home because I just can't—

Nine

They sprung Agnes and me from the infirmary in time for church. Reverend Cunkle preached a sermon against vanity, and Agnes and I made sour faces at each other over Hymn 497.

> *Come labour on.*
> *Who dares stand idle on the harvest plain,*
> *While all around him waves the golden grain?*
> *And to each servant does the Master say,*
> *"Go work today."*

It went on and on that way, advising that the enemy was watching night and day, and that no arm was so weak it couldn't do service.

Agnes scratched a note to me on her program. *This is*

WORSE than bloody faces! Blisters, backaches and callouses—icky! Let's become Buddhists!

After church I joined Cute Dibblee and her father. They were talking with APE on the church steps.

"This is the other girl having dinner with us, Pappy. This is Flanders Brown."

"Pleased to make your acquaintance," he said. Then, turning to APE, he said, "I'm real sorry the Cardmaker girl can't join us." He said it as though it was a question instead of a statement of fact.

Lorimer Will Dibblee was a medium-height man with a red, wrinkled face, brown curly hair, and brown eyes with thick eyebrows that met at the bridge of his nose. He wore a light gray suit with a bright yellow shirt and a matching yellow tie, and pigskin boots with gold buckles, and he carried a large white ten-gallon hat in his hand.

APE said, "Carolyn Cardmaker is being disciplined."

Will Dibblee sank one of his huge square hands into his pants pocket, rocked back on his heels, and drawled, "Well, who among us don't have sin, as the Bible says? Some of the greatest saints were sinners, ma'am. Moses murdered an Egyptian and hid him in the sand; David was an adulterer who took away the wives of three men; Jacob was a liar and a thief, deceived his blind and aging papa so he could get something didn't belong to him . . . and old Mary Magdalene was a hooker."

Cute's face went pale. I had to look away and concentrate on national disasters to keep from laughing. But the expression on APE's face didn't show signs of having heard anything of the kind.

"The girls must be back by three thirty for Quiet Hours," she said.

She went lumbering away in Billy's direction, and we three started down the hill to town.

"What's Cardmaker being disciplined for?" I said.

"You know the downstairs W.C., next to the gym?"

I nodded.

"Dance nights that's the boys' W.C. We're supposed to use the W.C. up on Bleak House. Last night Cardmaker and Butler Peabody were caught in the boys' W.C. Butler was trying to get this blue dye off Cardmaker's neck and back while your date, Cadet Thomas, kept guard. Miss Balfour caught them in there and thought Butler was taking down her straps."

"Where was Sumner when Miss Balfour showed up? Couldn't he warn them?" I said.

"She sneaked up on them," said Cute. "You know how sneaky she is. Now APE thinks they were trying to make out."

"The boy was just helping a damsel in distress," said Lorimer Will Dibblee. "Hell, that woman's got a dirty mind."

"Cardmaker is hall campused for six weeks," Cute said, "and she's lost her social privileges for the whole semester."

When we reached the Stonewall Jackson Hotel, I got my second glimpse of Cute Dibblee's tall, beautiful cousin. He had on the same white ducks with the blue denim jacket, his long wrists jumping past the jacket cuffs. He had the longest eyelashes I had ever seen, and he was smiling, showing his dimples, standing in front of a long, violet-colored Lincoln Continental, the type with porthole windows and a steel tire case on the back end. Across the door were the gold-printed words LORIMER

WILL DIBBLEE—*Montani Semper Liberi*. (Cute told me later that the Latin was the motto for the state of West Virginia: Mountaineers are always free men.)

"This here's my nephew," said Mr. Dibblee. "He's my sister's boy, and my sister, Cute's Aunt Hedda Fay, is a devout woman. She had herself three boys, then a girl, then another boy. She called them Matthew, Mark, Luke, Ann, John. This here's John."

He stepped forward with his hand outstretched. "John Dowder. Howdy."

"Hi. Flanders Brown," I said.

He grabbed my hand and squeezed it.

He was wearing something sweet-smelling and he had a blue cornflower in the lapel of his blue denim jacket. He walked alongside me as we went into the hotel, telling me he'd gone to Baptist church that morning because he was "a holy Baptist."

"Flanders, you're going to feel your eyes almost pop outta your head if you order one of the hotel steaks," he said as we crossed the lobby. "We ordered them last night and they come big as toilet seats!"

I swallowed hard and looked around to see if anyone had heard John Dowder bellow out that remark. No one seemed to care, if it had been heard. Ahead of us, Cute and her father were laughing and joking their way into the dining room.

"What do you do when you're home?" I said.

"I'm with the mine, same as Cute's pappy, but not rich as him yet. Off time I tend to the corn and strawberries we got in our patch. We got thirteen acres in our patch, so I keep going. I honey hunt some, too."

Everyone ordered a steak, and during lunch John explained honey hunting to me. You had to hike through brakes of wild honeysuckle, or trek down flower-fringed valleys, watching for wild bees, following them until you found old honey-holding post oaks. Then you built smoke fires of damp leaves or bits of punk to stupefy the bees, and you chopped out portions of the honey.

Mr. Dibblee was telling Cute a joke about a high Episcopalian minister who was always mistaken for a priest. The punch line was, "He's no Father, he's got four kids!" Mr. Dibblee said it loud enough for the whole dining room to hear, and a few people turned to look back at him.

Then Mr. Dibblee and John fooled back and forth swapping stories and smoking these big brown strong-smelling cigars, and I kept right on watching John's face. John was nineteen years old, the first older man I'd ever talked to that long who wasn't somebody's father or a neighbor, or someone who worked for my father.

I was wondering if it was really possible to fall in love with a face, and for no other reason. I was thinking about all the old popular songs about faces, with lines like ". . . and then I saw your fabulous face," . . . or "The first time ever I saw your face" . . . "Your looks are laughable, unphotographable, yet you're my favorite work of art."

The thing was, I was really moved by John Dowder, and I had been ever since I'd first laid eyes on him at the dance. Wheezing, short of breath, gasping for air, I'd seen that face across the gym and suddenly all that I'd heard about falling apart over someone's face didn't seem so impossible to believe anymore.

I liked a lot of the rest of him, too, how tall he was and the neat silky look his hair had, the way he smiled, the long eyelashes, the long farmer steps he took, and his certain way of throwing back his head to laugh. For no good reason I could figure out, I even liked those big smelly cigars.

The one thing I didn't like about him was the way he sometimes expressed himself. That made me cringe.

After Sunday dinner, he excused himself from the table for a while. When he came back, he said, "I thought something'd gone sour in the gents', till I remembered we all had asparagus for dinner."

He laughed very loud. So did Cute and her father.

"Let's face it," Cardmaker told me when I visited her, after I got back to school, "he's crude. The whole bunch is crude. Cute still hangs her underwear over the lampshades to dry, and it took all last year and a lot of demerits to get her to stop spitting. But so what? If you see something in him, what does it matter? You don't have to marry him! When you're thirty-six, he'll be *forty*, anyway! You have to think of things like that!"

"My skin crawls when he says some things," I said.

"Well, that's good exercise for your skin," said Cardmaker. "Anyway, I don't want to hear about someone falling in love when I'm hall campused, a social leper, and on report to my father. My father is going to hear that I was caught in a gym john with a cadet undressing me."

"It's lousy," I said, "particularly because I saw France Shipp making out with Peter Rider out on the playing field."

"She made a dive for Peter Rider the minute she heard Agnes had chickened out. She's so horny for Peter Rider it's gross," said Cardmaker. "Everybody knows they were making out all over the place. There's no justice."

"But won't your father believe you if you tell him the truth?"

"I'd have to tell him I'd dyed my formal," she said, "and I don't want to tell him that. He'd feel bad because he knows I don't have the clothes for this place. I told him my old costume for the Christmas pageant was just as good as any formal he could buy. Mom and I hate making him feel guilty because he can't give us things. He knew in his heart I needed a formal, that the Christmas pageant costume wasn't right, wouldn't last long if it was!"

I began to ponder the problem when Cardmaker said, "He'll be upset because I'm in trouble, too. It'll only reflect on him! And this is the wrong time for him to be upset, and for it to reflect on him!"

She was pacing up and down her room on Hard Times in an old seersucker bathrobe which had once belonged to Reverend Cardmaker. It was a man's knee-length which came to her toes. As she paced she wound a strand of her long blonde hair around one finger and told me there was a possibility her father was going to be moved to an even poorer parish in New Jersey. She said the trouble was he didn't get along with a certain Right Reverend Thomas Baird, D.D., LL.D., who took the "right" in his title literally. Cardmaker's father often pointed out things he was dissatisfied with.

"Old R.R. doesn't like any flak at all," said Cardmaker.

She flopped down on her bed. "I've made up my mind about something, Flanders."

"What?"

"I'm now an atheist. God doesn't give a damn and now I know it."

"If you know He doesn't give a damn, you can't be an atheist," I said. "According to atheists there isn't any God."

"There isn't!" she declared. "There's just a bunch of phonies living off stories of Jesus! Jesus was poor and he didn't own anything and he didn't even have a title, but look at the ones representing him today. Except for my father! They're all hustling to get the rich parishes with the big houses and long black cars, and they want to be the Right Reverend this and the Holiness that, and they're the most awful snobs you could ever see anywhere, Flanders! They all look down on my father because he's not chic or rich or all the rest of the crap they consider important. Well, I've had them and any God who lets them represent Him! I've had God!"

She stretched out with her arms behind her head and stared up at the ceiling. I realized for the first time that there were tears in her eyes. She was fighting for control.

She muttered, "Miss Blue's in trouble, too. I heard APE giving her hell for putting up that picture of Jesus in the john. I was waiting my turn to see APE and I heard her really giving it to Miss Blue."

I felt lousy that I had been the one to tell APE. She would have found out who'd done it, no doubt, but why did *I* have to tell her?

Cardmaker said, "That's what I mean about institutional religion! The really religious ones like Miss Blue get pushed around by the moneymaking rabble like APE! What's wrong with a picture of Jesus in the john?"

I said, "I was the one who made fun of it."

"That's your privilege," Cardmaker said. "Anyone who flaunts her religion all over the place has to take the chance someone else might not be tickled to death with the idea, but she should still have the right to flaunt it."

Cardmaker sat up and punched her palm with her fist. "I'm going to form an atheist club. Do you want to be a charter member?"

"I don't know. I have to think about it."

"If you have to think about it, I don't want you to be a charter member. I don't want any charter members who have to think about it."

"Then good luck," I said. "I have to get back to my room before Quiet Hours."

Cardmaker waved her hand at me like she was brushing debris out of the air.

I had a few minutes before Quiet Hours, time enough to make myself feel less to blame because I'd told APE who put up the picture of Jesus. I ran all the way to David Copperfield and knocked on Miss Blue's door.

"Yes, come in. Come in," she called out. "You're expected."

I tried the door but it was locked.

"Come in," she said. "I recognize you."

"I can't. The door's locked."

There was a moment's pause. Then she said, "Is someone there?"

"It's Flanders, Miss Blue."

After a few seconds, she unlocked the door, but she did not step back to let me enter. Over her shoulder I

87

could see a small narrow room, unadorned and neat like a nun's cell, with an even larger cross than the one she usually wore hanging over an iron bedstead like the ones in the infirmary.

"What is it, dear?" She seemed disappointed about something.

"I just wanted to say I never really minded the picture you put up in the john."

For a minute her eyes blinked rapidly. I could smell the gardenia fragrance. She said, "It's no longer in the W.C."

"I know. But I didn't mind it."

"It won't be put back, either."

"I wouldn't care if it was."

"It won't be."

"I'm sorry, Miss Blue."

She gave me one of her quick little automatic smiles, the sort that was more of a twitch than a smile. Then she closed the door gently while I was still standing there.

As I walked back to Little Dorrit, I wondered who she'd been expecting, or who she thought she'd recognized. I had never seen her in the company of other faculty members except in assembly or leaving a meeting. At night you often saw faculty members returning from the Star movie house in town, but Miss Blue was never among them. I had never heard her speak of a family or friends. I supposed that it had hurt her pride badly to be ordered to take down the picture. Perhaps she had also believed that Agnes or I had gone to APE about it.

By the time I got to Little Dorrit, I was so down I almost didn't see the black triangular sign hanging from

Agnes Thatcher's doorknob. The door was closed. Across the sign were large gold initials:

E. L. A.

Cardmaker had told me that when E.L.A. members recruited new people it was always done on Sunday during Quiet Hours. Two E.L.A.-ers simply walked to the prospect's room, hung the sign on the door, entered, and began whatever ritual was involved in soliciting someone. All of it was top secret, like what the initials stood for.

I sat on my bed and began a letter to my father just as the CLANG—DONG DONG began the hours officially. From my window I could see Miss Horton on her way to The Caravan for a smoke, and I believed that I could hear France Shipp's laughter coming from Agnes' room. I remembered its sound from breakfast the other morning.

I heard the sounds that Agnes made when she laughed, and I began to feel an intense dislike for the E.L.A., even though I was glad, I supposed, for Agnes' sake. Maybe it would make her feel more a part of things at Charles School.

But what right did they have to ruin Quiet Hours for everyone else by choosing that time for their membership calls? No one was supposed to talk during Quiet Hours, not even roommates! And what right did France Shipp have to make out with Peter Rider in the playing fields, on her honor not to go there for any reason but to let him have a smoke, while Cardmaker was in such trouble over a misunderstanding.

And most of all, what right did the E.L.A. have not to ask me?

Ten

Miss Blue's science class was the last class of the day. Only Miss Blue could hold anyone's attention at that hour, and her way of doing it was not as much teaching as it was dramatizing.

Take the afternoon in early November, for example, when Miss Blue began by walking across to the window, staring out for a while as though she'd forgotten we were there, and then without turning around to face us, she said, "On a cloudy, rainy day exactly like this one, in the year 1896, a Frenchman put something away in a drawer, until a sunny day should come along."

Then she turned and looked at us. "And because of just such a day as this, and because the Frenchman didn't know that he wouldn't need sunlight for what he'd planned, we had a discovery. What was it?"

"Was it radium?" Ditty Hutt asked.

"Not yet. It was a step in that direction."

"It was radioactive material," said Ditty, the only one who knew what Miss Blue was leading up to (because her father was a scientist); "it was Antoine Becquerel who put a piece of uranium ore in his desk drawer. He thought it was phosphorescent, and he wanted to see if when he exposed it to sunlight, he could use its light to make a photograph."

"Correct," said Miss Blue. "Becquerel put his carefully wrapped photographic plates into the desk drawer with the uranium ore. When a sunny day came, he took them out . . . and what did he discover?"

"He found the plates all fogged," said Ditty, "as if they'd been exposed to sunlight. He realized some kind of radiation was coming out of the ore, and it didn't matter if the ore had been exposed to sunlight or not."

Miss Blue then ran to the blackboard, her cross swinging back and forth across her bosom, while she drew the outlines of two large heads, a man's and a woman's. These were associates of Becquerel.

"They took over where he left off!" Miss Blue shouted excitedly. "Who will fill in their names?"

Before the hour and a half was up, there were not only the names of Pierre Curie and Marie Sklodowska Curie across the faces, there were formulas and dates drawn in various colors of chalk, and there were other outlines of faces, other names like Sir J.J. Thomson, Sir Ernest Rutherford, et cetera, and suddenly I knew about atoms and about alpha, beta, and gamma rays, and I'd even forgotten it was Miss Blue up there, crazy Miss Blue from the closet on David Copperfield, making *me*, hater of science and dunce about all things scientific, actually making me interested in all that.

It wasn't the first time it had happened. She'd also hooked me into listening about Newton's system with my mouth hanging open in wonder, as well as the theories of Copernicus, Galileo, and Archimedes. I wasn't the only one under Miss Blue's spell in the classroom; most of us came away with that sort of full, silent feeling that you have after you've seen a really good movie and you have to walk back out into the real world again.

My first view of the real world after that particular class was Cardmaker and Agnes Thatcher walking ahead of me. I couldn't figure out the two of them anymore. They spent a lot of time together. That was mostly due to the fact Cardmaker was hall campused, which meant she couldn't even leave Hard Times to go to Sweet Shoppe Queue after school, to go to town on Mondays ... or for any reason. And Agnes didn't like to go to town, didn't much like a lot of socializing, so they spent their time in Cardmaker's room on Hard Times. You could hear the raucous noises Agnes made when she laughed way down on Little Dorrit, when the two of them were together, and Agnes seemed to forgive Cardmaker anything.

Sometimes, for a joke, Cardmaker would reach out and suddenly pinch Agnes: in a class, in chapel, anywhere the atmosphere was placid. Agnes would always grab the spot where she'd been pinched and make a thunderous noise of protest like a banshee wailing. Whenever APE questioned her about it, Agnes always denied that she knew who the culprit was.

One time Cardmaker put a coat of colorless nail polish over Agnes' soap. That night when Agnes went in to take a bath, there were distinct sounds of frustration as she was unable to work up a lather, followed by angry noises growing louder, before the soap came flying across the bathroom. Cardmaker sneaked down to see it, bent double with laughter. When Agnes realized it was Cardmaker's trick on her, she only laughed along with Cardmaker.

If I had done it, it would have been worth several of her best bruising punches.

I had forgotten all about something Cardmaker had mentioned, and only that night in chapel did I notice something strange which brought it to mind.

I was standing beside Sue Crockett.

Cardmaker had become friends of sorts with Sue Crockett as well as Agnes. I saw Sue in her room sometimes after Sue came from town on Mondays. She would bring Cardmaker Milk Duds and Mallomars and bags of Fritos for snacks.

The first Wednesday of the new month was traditionally request night in chapel. Faculty members and students could request any hymn from Miss Able, who manned the organ.

Immediately Miss Mitchell raised her hand and requested #397.

We all rose and began singing, and Miss Mitchell stared hard in Miss Able's direction until Miss Able met her eyes.

> I look to thee in ev'ry need,
> And never look in vain;
> I feel thy strong and tender love,
> And all is well again;
> The thought of thee is mightier far
> Than sin and pain and sorrow are.

Everything was going along as always until suddenly I became aware of something odd during the singing of the second verse.

It was something Sue Crockett was doing, and I stopped singing myself, long enough to hear.

"Me in up springs heart new then And, thee of think only me let But."

I looked at her but she pretended she was singing the hymn no differently from anyone else. She looked back at me blankly.

For some reason I looked back at Agnes Thatcher. She was standing there holding the hymnal upside down.

I couldn't see Cardmaker. She was in the last row.

"Life quick'ning thy flows me Around," Sue was singing. I nudged her.

"Why are you singing it backwards?" I whispered.

"Because religion is backwards," she answered.

Then the bell in my memory which was trying to ring rang, and I remembered Cardmaker's vow to start an atheist club.

"How can you be an atheist when your mother owns a white Mercedes?" I said.

"A Mercedes has nothing to do with God."

"How can you *not* believe in God with all you have?" I persisted. "Atheism is for have-nots and malcontents."

"You know nothing about atheists," she said. "A lot of us are worth fortunes."

"Way your it have." I shrugged.

At the end of #397, APE huffed herself up to the podium and rasped out, "No talking during hymn singing!

94

How could you all be so rude! I'm sick in bed about it! Hear?"

Cute Dibblee requested #434, which was nothing more than "Mine eyes have seen the glory," and most everyone liked it and sang a rousing chorus of *Glory! Glory! Hallelujah!*

Still Sue persisted: *"On marching is truth His!"*

I caught up with Cardmaker later, in the line to Dombey and Son.

"I see your club is organized."

"You're pretty dense," she said. "We've been organized for weeks. We even rushed Agnes right under your nose."

"That was the reason for all the tricks then?"

"Join us," Cardmaker answered noncommittally, "unless you're afraid if you cease to believe you'll cease to behave."

"Who said anything like that?"

"That's what a lot of people think," she said. "People don't understand atheists."

"I think I do," I said. But I didn't tell her about my father. I decided against it—not just because we were in the dinner line and there wasn't time, but also because for some reason it embarrassed me. Even though Cardmaker might think it was really neat, I held back because I was ashamed of the fact.

"Why should *you* understand atheists?" she said. "Your life is without flak of any kind, so you believe."

"I have flak in my life," I said. Neither did I talk to Cardmaker about my mother.

"Oh really? What kind? A pimple on the chin in the

morning? An A minus instead of an A plus?" She looked up at the ceiling and rolled her eyes around as if to belittle everything about me. "It must be very hard on you."

"Cardmaker," I said, "what's the matter with you? We used to be pretty good friends, *I* thought."

"My mother's in the hospital," she said. "We can't afford it. I'm burned up at everything. My father's still in trouble. Life is a hole you fall down."

"I know it," I said.

"I'm glad you didn't say of all times I needed God more than ever," she said.

"I wouldn't say that."

"That's what Cute said," she said. "That dumb hillbilly!"

"What do you have to do to belong to your club?" I said.

"You have to actively oppose organized religion. You have to perform anti-organized religious tasks. I smell corned beef and cabbage," she said as the line moved.

"I'll think about it."

"We don't want anyone who has to think about it. I told you that. Every member also has to perform a major act of unfaith in order to become a full member."

"Like what?"

"I can't give examples," she said. "It gives too much of our secrets away. But each M.A.U. is assigned by me to the individuals."

"*You* decide what it's to be?"

"Yes."

"Do you want to eat at Miss Horton's?" I asked as the line moved more rapidly.

She shook her head. "We're all eating at Miss Balfour's

because we can plan things. She's always busy watching herself in the mirror."

I wasn't asked to join whoever "We're all" was supposed to be.

I ate at Miss Horton's table and over my shoulder noticed Cardmaker, Agnes, and Sue Crockett conferring together at the far end of Miss Balfour's table. No one else at the table seemed to be involved.

I figured that so far there were only three organized atheists at Charles.

After dinner I found two things in my mailbox. One was an invitation to the Thanksgiving Day Dance at Wales Military Academy. It was from Sumner Thomas. Attached to it was a poem.

> *You are enough bells*
> *And enough candles*
> *You are all the summer nights I can sleep*
> *And enough dreams.*

I had not seen or heard from Sumner Thomas since the night of my asthma attack, when he marched over for the dance.

The second message in my mailbox was a telegram.

TRY TO CATCH ME ON TELEVISION TONIGHT
AT 9:30 CONTROVERSY CHANNEL 6
LOVE DAD

Eleven

At nine fifteen, armed with a permission slip from APE herself, I left study hall to go to Tale of Two Cities. Agnes Thatcher accompanied me, since APE insisted that an E.L.A. member must be in my company while I watched my father on television in Billy's sitting room.

(If it strikes you odd that Agnes Thatcher was both an Extra Lucky Ass and a member of Cardmaker's atheist club, it struck me that way, too.)

Billy was the only person at Charles School allowed television. It was claimed that he watched only the news and certain erudite specials on the boob tube, but there were other claims that any afternoon at all between one and four, the soap operas were in process along T. of T.C.

Billy seemed really delighted to have company, and he

had already placed two large leather chairs before the tube, with a small table between them. On the table were glasses and two Coke bottles resting atop some chipped ice in a silver wine bucket.

He was dressed to the teeth, as usual, and the glitter from his Phi Beta Kappa key, strung across his pinstriped vest, was so bright it was impossible not to imagine that he had shined it for the occasion.

I never figured out whether Agnes' presence was because APE thought it would protect Billy from me, or me from Billy, but Agnes had been her usual ungracious self about the request. When I'd asked her, at the beginning of study hall, she'd held her nose with two fingers of one hand, and reached up to flush with the other—the familiar gesture.

Billy was the only adult at Charles who perceived that it was not necessary to act out in pantomime whatever it was he wanted to communicate to Agnes. He didn't shout at her, either.

He asked us both if we wanted some Ritz crackers to go with our Cokes, and he apologized because he didn't have anything to put on them. He said he was supposed to be on a diet, and he wasn't supposed to interfere with our rules and regulations. I had the idea that all the while he was making this little speech, he had a Sara Lee chocolate cake in his freezer (there was a compact refrigeration/freezer unit next to a small sink and petit stove, in a far corner of the room, partially hidden by a screen). I believed he had a box of Barton's liqueur-filled bonbons in the top drawer of his large oak desk, too. He was no less terrified of APE than all of us, I believed.

There wasn't much small talk before the program started.

This is how it went:

TRIPP: This is James Tripp and the name of this show, as you know, is *Controversy*. Good evening, viewers, and good evening to my guest, Mr. Theodore Brown. Or is it *Dr.* Brown?

BROWN: Good evening.

TRIPP: Is it Mr. Brown or Dr. Brown?

BROWN: It's Mr. Brown. You can call me Ted.

TRIPP: Then it isn't Dr., after all, even though your business seems to be some form of healing?

BROWN: I don't think of myself as a healer. The people who come to me are not sick. They're seeking something, which is why we call them seekers.

TRIPP: Ah, yes, the seekers. At one hundred and fifty dollars a weekend and up. And you are *not* a doctor. You do not even have a degree in psychology, do you, Mr. Brown?

BROWN: No, I don't have a degree in psychology. Neither did Sigmund Freud, if I may be bold enough to insert his name in these proceedings.

TRIPP: But Sigmund Freud *was* a doctor. An M.D.!

BROWN: A biologist, if I recall accurately. He was not trained in the field he entered and excelled in. He was not confined to a limited area of inquiry.

TRIPP: And you certainly aren't, either, are you, Mr. Brown? For example, your experiments in human sexuality.

BROWN: Yes. Certainly human, not bestial.

TRIPP: You're a very flip fellow, *Mis*-ter Brown. Perhaps it's a cynicism derived from skipping about from field to field. At one time you were actually doing readings, weren't you, of people's handwriting?

BROWN: The study of graphology is perfectly legitimate.

TRIPP: I suppose as legitimate as tea-leaf reading, wouldn't you say?

BROWN: I haven't done any tea-leaf reading. I think you should inquire more about Attitudes, Inc., which is our main endeavor. We have a group of—

TRIPP: *Mis*-ter Brown, I'm the host here, and if there are any speeches to be made, I'll make them.

BROWN: I thought you were going to extend the guest the courtesy of describing his present work, that's all.

TRIPP: I will, *Mis*-ter Brown, just as soon as I let the listener put my guest's past in perspective. . . . For example, *Mis*-ter Brown, in your various *experiments* with sexuality, isn't it true that your own wife participated with a young research assistant, and that your wife left you—as did the research assistant?

BROWN: The fact is—

TRIPP: The fact is, *Mis*-ter Brown, if Brown is your real last name, the fact is you specialize in phony setups which feature very loose morality and, in plain words, provide facilities for people who indulge in ob—

That was as far as Mr. Tripp got before Billy trotted rapidly across the room and turned off the set.

"I think we've had enough *controversy*, don't you?"

I said yes, but I couldn't look him in the eye, and I couldn't look at Agnes, either.

Billy said, "Those programs hire hosts that do everything to antagonize their guests, including lying about them. They try to be suspenseful, but they invariably result in bad taste."

I didn't say anything.

"It was very pleasant having you here all the same," Billy said.

"Lo leet you," said Agnes.

"Yes, well, I'm glad you could come," he said.

"Gite," said Agnes, and we both started walking toward the door.

Agnes opened it and started out and I started after her. Billy said, "Flanders?"

I said "What?" without turning around to look at him. I just stood there with my back to him and my head down.

"Flanders, Freud *was* a biologist. Your father was right. And he did a lot of experimenting where others thought he shouldn't. At one time he even got himself addicted to cocaine. Flanders?"

"What, sir?"

"It's all right."

"No, it's not, sir," I said. "Most of that junk is true. I guess it all is. I guess when *Mrs.* Ettinger hears I'll be sent home."

Agnes was standing outside waiting for me. I still hadn't looked at her face.

Billy came up around me and stood before me. He looked up at me and said, "I won't tell Mrs. Ettinger, if you'd prefer. But it wouldn't matter. We didn't enroll your father. We enrolled you."

I said thank you. I was remembering the perspiration that began to dot my father's forehead when it began getting rough for him.

"My father means well," I said, because I honestly felt that, even after what I had heard, even while I was still in the process of perceiving so many things—why the advanced therapy was always in another building, why we sometimes received obscene telephone calls I was always told to hang up on *instantly* . . . and even why my father didn't really want me for weekends in the new Maryland place. I would only be in the way of all that sort of thing, without my mother to keep an eye on me, and me not knowing anyone in town to fill my time with. I would only be underfoot.

Billy said, "Remember something, Flanders, about the Mr. Tripps in this world: When someone goes out to beat a dog, he can always find a stick."

"Good night, sir," I said.

"Not that your father is to be compared with a dog," Billy said. "It's simply an old saying."

But I was thinking in a lot of ways he was a dog, a dirty dog if it was true that he had involved my mother in— I couldn't finish the thought. I wanted to push it out of the way.

She'd never had a mind of her own. I'd always remember her mouthing his opinions, beginning most of her sentences with "Ted says" and "According to Ted—"

I felt Agnes sock me in the shoulder as I stepped out onto Tale of Two Cities. She hurt me and it even felt good—probably saved me from having another little accident, I thought; light into me, Agnes.

"Dand!" she shouted. That was my name in Agnesthatcher.

I looked at her and she had a furious expression. She made her nose pug to imitate the snub-nosed Mr. Tripp.

Then she made the motions of a prizefighter, dancing around punching an opponent.

Much later that night, long after light bell, when I returned from the infirmary after another injection of epinephrine to quiet an asthma attack, I found a note on my floor which Agnes had pushed under my door.

What did you do to deserve tonight? What did any of us do to deserve things? Aren't you ready to join AAAC?

Unfaithfully, A.T.

P.S. Your father's great-looking!

I wasn't ready to become an atheist yet, not because I believed that much in God, but because I didn't believe that much in my father anymore. Not enough to want to be what he was.

Twelve

On the way to Wales Military Academy for the Thanksgiving Day Dance, I sat beside Miss Sparrow on the bus. She was a redhead like me, with freckles and blue eyes like me. I hoped I wouldn't end up like her, for she had an air of tragedy about her. She taught drama and smelled of strong Turkish cigarettes, and she was the only member of the faculty who dressed with a great deal of style. She wore fur-lined capes, and scarves with large bold patterns, hats with feathers, and fantastic shoes with toes and heels carved out, wedgies, slippers, a vast assortment. When she wasn't in The Caravan, where it was rumored she chain-smoked sixteen cigarettes at one sitting, she was in her room reciting scenes from plays into her tape recorder. Everyone said she was secretly in love with Reverend Cunkle, and he with her, and just to be near him she had given up all her Broadway dreams. He was married, with a family of four, and lived across from Charles School opposite St. Thomas church. About the only time they saw each other was during play rehearsals, since he took an active interest in anything theatrical.

"Are you excited?" she asked me.

I wasn't. I was wishing Sumner Thomas was Cute's cousin, John Dowder, for one thing! For another, there is definitely something unexciting about an afternoon tea dance.

"I'm not too excited," I said. "Were you, when you were my age, at dances and things?"

"I was a drama bug," she said. "I had no time for silly boys."

"Not ever?"

"Seldom," she relented. "I went to high school with Ernestine, and she was the one the boys chased."

"Miss Blue?"

"Yes."

"*Our* Ernestine Blue?"

"Our Ernestine Blue. 'Nesty.'"

"'Nesty.'" I repeated the nickname, trying to conjure up some image of Miss Blue which would fit with this new information.

I said, "I never thought you were that old."

"How old do you think I am?"

"I thought you were about thirty-five, but I thought Miss Blue was at least twenty years older!"

"I'm thirty-nine. She's a little over forty."

"Miss Blue?"

"Our Miss Blue," she assured me.

"Well, I wonder what happened to her?" I said, and as I said it, the driver of the bus shouted out, "WALES!" We were there. With a great *whoosh* the front door of the bus opened.

Before I got up, I turned to Miss Sparrow. "What happened to Miss Blue?" I said.

"I lost track of her after high school. Her family moved to Kentucky."

"You know what I mean," I said.

"*What* do you mean?" she said.

"I mean look at her now."

"Everyone changes," Miss Sparrow said.

"And you're not friends now?"

"I didn't say we weren't friends now."

But they weren't, even though she didn't say they weren't. No one was friends with Miss Blue so far as I knew.

I decided to tell Sumner about it; it was a strange and mysterious story, and I would ask him what he made of it. It was also a good opener.

We stood around outside the Wales gym while I told him, watching the others file in, watching buses of girls arrive from Mary Baldwin and Miss Fern's and Virginia Mountain School.

"Well?" I said when I finished. "What do you make of Miss Blue?"

"I'm going to recite my newest to you," he said.

"Don't you care about anything I said?"

"Hush," he said. "See what you think of it." He took a deep breath. Then he recited:

Rooms I've loved I've left and houses, cities, worlds,

You I could not leave.
I love your face. I love your face.

He turned to see the expression on my face. "Well?" he said.

I said, "It's very nice. But."

"But what?"

"But why is it to *me*? It isn't to *me*! You haven't even written me or called me since September!"

"I sent you a poem with the invitation, didn't I?"

"Sumner," I said, "we don't even know each other. You don't love my face!"

"Don't be so literal!" he said.

"If you think I'm enough bells and candles and you love my face so much, how come you won't even listen when I want to tell you a good story?"

"Shhhhh, Flanders," he said. "You're going to spoil Thanksgiving."

While we danced around and drank a really sweet cider punch, I kept remembering John Dowder. After he got back to West Virginia he'd written Cute a thank-you note. He'd spelled forward "fourword," surprise "suprise," and sincerely "cinserly," and his handwriting had run across the page uphill. According to my father's old handwriting analyses, uphill writing was a sign of cockeyed optimism, or "false euphoria." I didn't care. And he signed his letter, "Yours till the creek runs dry, John."

Sumner talked about suicide a lot during slow numbers. I was learning that was his favorite subject. He rattled on about a book he was going to write called *Killing Yourself Successfully*, because it was not as easy as it seemed.

He told me that when the famous artist Arshile Gorky did himself in, he hung nooses all over his Connecticut property until he got the nerve to put his head through one.

"I'd jump," he confided to me near the end of the dance as we walked through the W.M.A. stables where he showed me the horse he always rode. "Even though that's supposed to mean you feel you've fallen from favor. It's still a very sure way."

"Who said it meant that?"

"This shrink named Stekel. He killed himself, too, after he made a study of suicide. He swallowed 22 bottles of ordinary aspirin," said Sumner. "How would you do it, Flanders?"

"Pills," I said. "I'd like to just never wake up if I was going to do it."

"Females are pill takers," he said. He stopped before a black horse and hugged its head. "Men have used guns, traditionally, and females used to wade out and drown. But then, thanks to Seconal, Librium, Doriden, et cetera . . ."

I didn't ask him how his mother had done it, though I wanted to.

Sumner was talking to the horse next. "Life is a fatal disease, isn't it, Ebony?"

Then suddenly Sumner grabbed me and pulled me against him to kiss me. It was one of those French numbers I'd heard about.

There was nothing sexy about it, as far as I was concerned. I wanted to go back to Charles and boil my mouth.

Miss Sparrow's voice was shouting, "Pass through but don't pause in the stables!"

"We'd better head for the buses," I said to Sumner.

He shrugged and walked ahead of me slowly, kicking the dirt lightly with his boot and keeping his head down. I noticed a run in my panty hose, and worried that it had been there all afternoon.

When we all returned to Charles, there was a rumor circulating that someone had written out the meaning of E.L.A. on the study-hall blackboard. A faculty member had seen it there and erased it. Everyone was gossiping about it, but no one seemed to know what exactly was supposed to have appeared on the blackboard.

APE was away from school for the long weekend, and whoever would have to pay for the deed would have to wait.

I changed from my best dress to a second best, and borrowed a pair of panty hose from Agnes' top drawer. She was not around, and I guessed she was hanging out with Cardmaker. I went off to the line for Dombey and Son, looking for Cute. Cute and I were just about the only girls who didn't belong to some secret club.

We were last in line. When we got inside, we had to sit at Miss Blue's table.

She waited for everyone to quiet down before she began grace.

Then she said, "He that hath an ear, let him hear. . . . Amen."

I stared at Miss Blue in amazement, and Cute did, too. Perhaps this short grace was in honor of Thanksgiving; I nudged Cute and suggested the idea. Cute shrugged.

France Shipp was at our table, and so was Ditty Hutt.

While the other tables were filled, ours was not. Several girls had gone home for the holiday.

Everyone at the table was exchanging glances, marveling at the brevity of Miss Blue's grace. She seemed not to notice. Mechanically she wiped her hands off after passing things, and filled her plate with healthy portions of the usual Thanksgiving fare. There was a slight film over the baked candied sweet potato, and Miss Blue was oblivious to Ditty Hutt's suggestion that it was loaded with saltpeter.

I finally spoke up. "I didn't know you went to school with Miss Sparrow, Miss Blue."

"Did you, Miss Blue?" Cute said.

She gave us one of her flickering smiles and nodded. Then back to her own little world.

Cute said, "Are we going to have a test tomorrow, Miss Blue?"

Another flickering smile, a nod in the negative.

France Shipp and Ditty Hutt were talking about the snow reports, and I tried a *sotto voce* conversation with Cute to fill her in on what Miss Sparrow had told me about Miss Blue.

It was right at that point that we all heard Miss Blue say, "I talked to Jesus, and He knew I knew He was there."

She said it in such a dreamy voice that I had thought for a moment she was starting to sing a song, but she wasn't. The others simply stared at her; no one said anything.

Then France Shipp said, "What was that, Miss Blue?"

Miss Blue had stopped eating. She touched her napkin

to the corners of her mouth, placed it back in her lap, flicked her smile at us, and said, "Jesus was in my room this afternoon."

Ditty Hutt hunched over in an attempt to gain control, clapping her palms to her mouth. Cute began twisting her napkin in her lap, staring straight down at her plate. I tried to concentrate on national disasters.

France Shipp spoke up again in her best supercool voice. "Oh, was He up on David Copperfield?"

Miss Blue's head was shaking slightly as she spoke and her voice trembled. "He was with me."

"Where is He now, I wonder," said France. I suddenly didn't have to worry that I would laugh aloud. I was beginning to feel sorry for Miss Blue, and hateful toward France Shipp.

Ditty Hutt's shoulders were shaking.

"Excuse me, girls," said Miss Blue. "You are on your honor to leave when you are all finished. I must go to chapel and pray."

"Run along, Miss Blue, and don't worry," said France Shipp. "You must have had quite an afternoon."

Miss Blue rose and skirted out of Dombey and Son, looking neither left nor right, rushing along, as our table burst into laughter. I laughed, too, partly because I thought it was funny, and partly because I was relieved to have Miss Blue out of France Shipp's cool hands. I could not help remembering that Miss Blue was only around forty, not old and strange from living too long, but strange for some other reason; pretty once with all the boys after her, and now living in a cleared-out closet of a girls' boarding school without any friends.

I had the feeling if I laughed any longer I'd have some terrible punishment inflicted on me, because I had the feeling what I was doing was cruel. My father had told me once that often if you did something cruel, you hurt yourself, had a trivial accident, or missed an appointment you looked forward to—as a way of making yourself pay for the cruelty. ("But there is no God up there deciding you're not going to get this because you did that!" he'd told me.)

With my accident-proneness for starters, I was surely headed for broken limbs and total paralysis, and I sat there morbidly contemplating this while the others began calming down.

Toward the end of our meal, Miss Horton's table filed out of the dining room. Suddenly there was a shrill cry that sounded like "Danny! Danny!" It came closer and closer and stopped in front of me.

"Danny" was Agnesthatcher for panty hose. Agnes was crouched down, pointing at my legs and screaming.

When I got back to my room on Little Dorrit, there was a note waiting for me in her handwriting. *Those were my good Christian Dior panty hose I was saving for a special occasion! I intend to get even! Not tomorrow or the next day, maybe, but someday. You will know when I do! A.T.*

Before I fell asleep I pondered the reason I hadn't had an asthma attack after my visit to the stables with Sumner. Maybe animal dander hadn't caused the first attack. Maybe it was just soul dander, when your own soul just got fed up and gave off something like dandruff to show you.

On Sunday after APE returned, the culprit who had written out the meaning of E.L.A. in study hall was uncovered. It was Agnes Thatcher.

No one else could figure out why she would do such a thing, but Cardmaker told me why. It was Cardmaker's idea; it was Cardmaker's assignment—Agnes' Major Act of Unfaith.

For the first time in 150 years at Charles School, everyone came to know that all E.L.A. meant was Episcopal Library Association.

Thirteen

Dear Flan-Tan,
I'm sorry that the television show embarrassed you. I admit that I didn't realize how low he'd punch. I would not have consented had I known. BUT: You must realize by now that anyone in my position is subject to criticism, distortion, sarcasm, et cetera. Do you remember how Tripp tried to imply my last name might not be Brown? "Mr. Brown, if that's really your last name—"

Not everything was true, at all, but sex is a part of our inquiry and a legitimate one. Don't always think of sex as something dirty or you're going to be sadly disappointed with a fair percentage of your love life. . . . As for your mother's participation—she was my associate. Ask her, Flan, if it seems important. You should be in touch with her anyway.

I hope we can schedule a visit soon, for I'm anxious to have you look over the place. But it is almost Christmas, isn't it? I miss you terribly.

Love,
Dad

P.S. We'll spend Christmas in Auburn with Grandma Brown. You can see your old friends. Okay?

I had slipped around a corner outside study hall to read the letter from my father. Just as I was finishing it, I saw Miss Able pull Miss Mitchell into the same corner, a little ahead of me. Miss Able slammed her against the wall and snarled ". . . ever forget that part of it!"

Miss Mitchell was ripping something into pieces and crying.

Did either one see me? I doubt it. It was all over almost as quickly as it had started. I was alone there. I could hear the students beginning to pour into study hall for evening hours. I took a last look at my father's letter and tore it up, noticing whatever it was Miss Mitchell had torn up ahead of me on the floor. I walked over and picked up pieces of a photograph. There was Miss Able's ear and half of her face. I bent down and picked up the rest, putting all the ripped things into the wastebasket near the water fountain.

CLANG—DONG DONG made the start of study hall official.

"Dand!" I saw Agnes waving at me as I entered, indicating that she'd saved me a seat.

"Flanders?" I saw Cute pointing to the seat beside hers.

On my way to accept Agnes' offer, I stopped to explain to Cute, "Agnes was really mad at me because I borrowed her panty hose without asking. She was swearing revenge. I think I'll let her make up with me. Okay?"

Cute said, "Okay. But I still think what she did was lousy. E.L.A. didn't force her to join. What'd she join for, just to expose them?"

"She says she's against clubs like that and they should be exposed."

"Big possums climb little trees," said Cute.

"Take your seats!" Miss Able's voice rang out.

I hurried into the one Agnes was saving for me. "Thanks," I whispered as she watched my lips. "I'm glad you didn't stay mad long. You need all the friends you can get."

She stuck out her tongue and made an obscene gesture with her fist.

Agnes wasn't a big hero around Charles School since she had exposed the Extra Lucky Asses. Some of the students equated it with breaking nuns' vows and worse. But there were just enough of us who appreciated what she'd done to exalt her to a sort of minor hero. I secretly think some of the faculty were for her, too: Miss Horton, for one. I had a hunch she'd seen France Shipp that night out on the playing fields with Peter Rider. I had a feeling Miss Horton didn't think certain girls should be more privileged than others any more than I did, any more than a small but very vocal and aggressive group of others did. We were the ones who delighted in discovering that essentially E.L.A. had been formed so the library would be tended, and that their motto was *O sancta simplicitas! (O sacred simplicity!)*. Cardmaker said she had this big picture of them summers, stretched out on the decks of their yachts while they sailed around the Greek islands, murmuring to themselves, *"O sancta simplicitas!"* Cardmaker always had very definite visual images where The Rich were concerned. They were in places like "their drawing room," "their library," "their Rolls-Royce"; or they were "on their way to the stock market," or "on their way to a huge costume ball overlooking a canal in Venice," or "just coming back from safari."

"Cardmaker," I would protest, "not every Extra Lucky Ass is a millionaire."

"Those that aren't are 'old names,' " said Cardmaker. "They're even worse. There was a bishop I remember named Pilling from Philadelphia. Pilling is one of the 'old names' in Philadelphia. This Bishop Pilling got everything handmade, even his shoes, but he never had to pay for them because he said his wearing them was a good advertisement. 'Old names' are always up to things like that, hanging out at the Ritz without paying for it, and other gross things, just because they're 'old names.' They're parasites."

"SILENCE! SIIIIII-LENCE!" Miss Able was literally screaming, with her eyes bulging from their sockets.

Out of the side of my mouth I tried to warn Agnes that she was in a foul mood, but there wasn't any way for her to read my lips.

Everyone shut up and opened books, and for a long while you couldn't hear anything but the turning of pages and the scratching of pens and pencils. Miss Able herself was writing page after page on light blue stationery, bent over her task with utter concentration. I remembered that just that evening before dinner she had begun chapel with hymn #489: "Blest Be the Tie that Binds." What had happened between chapel and study hall?

As I was wondering this, Agnes Thatcher suddenly jumped to her feet, holding her bottom and crying out in one of her loudest banshee wails. I looked up amazed to see that the hand not holding the bottom was pointing at me.

"Deuce!" she complained.

Translated from Agnesthatcher, "deuce" was "goose," and Agnes Thatcher had her revenge. Everyone in study hall, including a wild-eyed, feet-stamping Miss Able, was sure I had goosed Agnes while she was quietly studying.

"She's lying," I protested to Miss Able.

"Go directly to Mrs. Ettinger's office with this note," Miss Able answered, writing something across a piece of notepaper.

"She *is* lying, though," I said, wanting desperately to avoid this confrontation with APE. "You have to believe me. I mean, look what she did to E.L.A."

But Miss Able was still in the very foul mood she'd been in when study hall had begun. "Hurry! Out of my sight!" she ordered.

As I passed Agnes, she had her head in an E-Lit book, her eyes refusing to look in my direction. I just hoped she could feel my vibrations; I was sending them straight at her, loud and clear.

Miss Able's note said:

I cannot keep discipline with Flanders Brown present. She pinched Agnes Thatcher in order to make her cry out and disrupt study hall!   Ellen Able

It was a very whiny-sounding note. I think APE thought so too, for she spent very little time reprimanding me, beyond the predictable announcement that I was to forfeit all the Mondays until Christmas. (So much for Christmas shopping, I brooded. I'd be left behind with Cardmaker and Agnes for company!)

Then The Inquisition began.

"Flanders, you're an intelligent girl, and Miss Blue is your faculty chum. What do you think of her health?"

"Her health is fine, I suppose."

"Do you know what I mean by her health?"

"How she feels?"

"Physically and *mentally*."

"She feels fine, as far as I know."

"According to France Shipp you were present at the dinner table on Thanksgiving when Miss Blue mentioned speaking with Jesus."

"Yes, ma'am."

"Well?"

"She's very religious," I said.

"Flanders, I'm not questioning that. I'm simply concerned for Miss Blue. I don't think she's herself lately. Putting up a picture of Jesus in the W.C. and so forth."

"As far as I know her, that's like her," I said.

"Do you take her afternoon class or her morning class?"

"Afternoon, ma'am."

"Was she up to par today, for example?"

"Yes. She was very up to par. We learned about snob gases."

"I *beg* your pardon?"

"Snob gases," I said. "Gases that refuse to combine with anything else under any conditions." I suddenly thought of something which had not occurred to me before. Was Miss Blue slyly putting in her own two cents about the E.L.A. matter? It was the main topic of the day, after all; it had been for over a week. And Miss Blue had inserted into her lesson that while Cavendish, their discoverer, had called them "noble gases" because of their elite quality, she preferred to think of them as "the snobs."

APE was frowning and rubbing her chins with her great chunky fingers. "Snob gases?"

"Argon and neon, for example. They're used to light advertising signs."

"Let's get back to the subject," said APE, who I could tell didn't know anything about gases of any kind. "Have you ever heard Miss Blue talking to herself in her room?"

"I don't live near her," I said. "But I've heard Agnes Thatcher carrying on in *her* room."

"We're not talking about Agnes Thatcher," APE said. "Yet."

"Miss Blue seems fine in every way to me," I said.

"France Shipp said she called on her after Thanksgiving dinner, to make sure she was all right, and Miss Blue was in her room, with her door closed, chanting."

"Maybe she was praying," I said.

"Aloud?"

I said, "Maybe."

"France Shipp said she was chanting."

"Well, praying could sound like chanting," I said.

"Flanders, I think you know what I'm getting at. It's very noble to defend your faculty chum, if that's what you imagine you're doing, but you should be sick in bed about signs she's clearly evincing of having some mental disturbance!"

"I didn't know that, ma'am."

"*You* knew that."

"I really didn't."

"But you and Carolyn Cardmaker and the like are intent on being the misdemeanists."

"Not me," I said.

"Not *I*," she corrected me.

"Not I. I'm not intent on being a misdemean anything. I just like Miss Blue a lot and think she's an excellent teacher."

"We're not on that subject anymore."

"What subject are we on?"

"Carolyn Cardmaker," APE said.

"I like her, too," I said.

"You more than like her, I would say. You bend to her will."

"I don't, ma'am, and that's the truth."

"You and the rest of her lackeys," she continued, ignoring my protestation. "You and poor Agnes Thatcher. Now Agnes Thatcher didn't decide of her own volition to make public disclosures concerning the E.L.A. Any fool in long pants knows that much. Agnes Thatcher hasn't got a mean bone in her body!"

"Ma'am?" I said incredulously.

"She doesn't. Now, she doesn't, and I don't want any

more mendacity and subterfuge on the subject! A poor child like that does not spend her hours plotting and conniving the way a Carolyn Cardmaker does!" APE was highly upset, rubbing her diamond like crazy, her eyes practically putting out sparks. "You pinch the poor child when she's trying to study, and Carolyn Cardmaker poisons the child's mind! I never knew such unkind girls before. I never dreamed in my wildest imaginings that this brand of cruelty could exist here in Charles School. It is your *duty* to *help* Agnes!"

I couldn't think of anything to say, much less to try and convince APE I wouldn't even be there if Agnes hadn't been just as capable of plotting and conniving as the rest of us.

APE said, "Go to your room. Don't go back to study hall this evening. Go to your room immediately, and have your lights off in ten minutes. Do you understand?"

"Yes, ma'am."

"Emerson said in his essay 'Manners': *A beautiful behavior is better than a beautiful form; it gives a higher pleasure than statues or pictures; it is the finest of the fine arts.*"

"Yes, ma'am. I never knew he said that, ma'am."

"Think about it! And this: *So nigh is grandeur to our dust, So near is God to man,*"—I had to look away from her, her voice was shaking so—"*When Duty whispers low,* Thou must, *The youth replies,* I can." She stood up and, glaring at me, demanded, "Who wrote *that*?"

"Shakespeare?"

"Ralph Waldo Emerson!" she bellowed back, as though she had triumphed over me in some sort of contest of wills, wits, whatever.

Our interview was over. APE stormed away, leaving me to make my way up to Little Dorrit.

When I came to the top of the stairs on David Copperfield, I saw Miss Blue sitting in her usual spot, under the picture of Mary, Queen of Scots. She was reading the Bible, open at Revelations.

I said, "I have another Revelation for you, Miss Blue. I've been sent from study hall. Mrs. Ettinger has me campused on Mondays until Christmas, and I have to have my lights out immediately."

"What did you do to deserve all that, dear?"

"I have to have my lights out practically immediately," I said, "so I'll tell you tomorrow." Then I said, "Miss Blue?"

"Yes, Flanders?"

"Did snob gases have anything to do with E.L.A.?"

Her flickering smile, the slight blush to her cheeks. "Dear, you haven't time. Practically immediately is almost past."

"You're okay, Miss Blue," I said.

She nodded her head, murmuring something that sounded vaguely like "Amen," "I am," or "My friend."

I never knew which.

Fourteen

It was a few Sundays before Christmas, and there was a tree trimmed in gold and silver on the altar at church.

As we marched down the aisle at the end of the service, Cardmaker was singing: *"Eternal King O, on Lead, come has march of day The—"*

"Henceforth in fields of conquest," I was singing right along, *"Thy tents shall be our home."*

"Preparation of days Through," Cardmaker sang.

"Thy grace has made us strong," I tried to drown her out.

"Eternal King O, now And—"

"We lift our battle song."

Before we launched into the second verse, I nudged Cardmaker in the side. "Aren't you going to let up for Christmas?" I asked.

"Let up for Christmas?" she said. "That's the time when we're most appropriate! Christmas hasn't got anything to do with God! It's all one big hard sell!"

"Hush! Girls!" Miss Balfour turned around to raise a scolding finger. "Sing!" She was wearing a piece of mistletoe attached to her hat, and she had two round balls of rouge on her cheeks which looked like tree decorations.

Everything at Charles School was taking on a festive air. There was fake snow on the windows and tinsel hanging from plants, and there were wreaths with red bows and clumps of evergreen branches tied with colored ribbon resting on tables and over pictures in the hallways.

There was an air of excitement, too; things seemed to be in an up-tempo, everyone was busy, lively. The news was being passed that France Shipp was no longer wearing her two-carat diamond ring, and certain afternoons from the windows on Bleak House you could see her huddled in one of her heavy woolen sweaters, sitting beside Peter Rider in the gazebo on South Lawn, while the leaves blew around them in a storm.

A townie was writing to Agnes. He had seen her several times at church. "I love how you look," he had written in his first letter. "I know you're deaf. I made inquiries. I hope you don't mind! I couldn't help myself!" He said he was sixteen, attended local high school, wanted to be a veterinarian, and hoped Agnes would invite him to call.

Agnes did. She wrote back that he was welcome in her room on Little Dorrit anytime he could find a way to get there. Since she was room campused, except to attend classes, chapel, study hall, meals and church, he would please plan his visit for sometime after light bell or in the early hours before dawn "when your presence along the halls will be less noticeable."

His name was Stephen Woolwine. He began writing once a week, then two and three times, delighting in Agnes' sassy responses. She began squirming in her seat Sundays, trying to pick him out of the crowd, but he refused to help her or give her any clues. He would remain a mystery man, he wrote, until she could meet him face to face.

The drama club was rehearsing *The Importance of Being Earnest*, with Ditty Hutt in the lead male role as Algernon. She was running around the halls in silk knickers reciting lines like "Piano playing is not my forte," while all of us pumped her on what exactly went on between Reverend Cunkle and Miss Sparrow. Reverend Cunkle was directing the play.

"They just crack up over anything the other one says," Ditty said.

Miss Sparrow was wearing out a bright red velvet suit, showing up in it at every rehearsal; around her neck was a black velvet ribbon with a gold key attached to it.

"It's a new gold key," Ditty Hutt told us. "I've heard he gives her a gift at the beginning of every new venture they get involved in."

"Keep your eyes peeled," Cardmaker advised her. "We want a full report."

"I don't think anything goes on between them," said Ditty. "I just think they turn each other on and that's it."

"Keep your eyes peeled anyway," Cardmaker said.

Cardmaker was mad at everyone Episcopal, particularly the clergy. Her father had written that it would probably be the family's last Christmas in Union, that he was being assigned to a smaller parish about 90 miles from Union.

"You can't get much smaller than Union," she had complained. "You practically don't exist at all if you're smaller than Union!"

That morning as we marched from church together, she was dressed inappropriately for the weather. She was wearing a lightweight corduroy jacket over a black nylon drip-dry dress, panty hose, heels, and a black felt beanie on her head.

After the hymn, as we were slowly filing out, I showed her the newest poem sent to me by Sumner Thomas.

You are words like "toward," "in," "here," "yes,"
  "now," "come," and "part of."
I am sliding.
You are "hush," "dear," "oh!," "open," "touch."
I am sliding.
You are "darling"
(I can)
"always"
(not)
"love me"
(hold)
"dearest"
(out)
"my"
(much)

"beloved"
(longer)
I am a word like yours.

Cardmaker handed back the piece of Wales stationery with the poem written across it. Underneath Sumner had scribbled "Another one for you, Flanders."

"He likes to write poetry." Cardmaker shrugged. "What's wrong with that? There are heads of state planning ways to suck money out of the pockets of the poor, and you meet a boy who likes to write poetry—what's wrong with that?"

"Cardmaker, don't always bring the world into matters," I said. "There's nothing wrong with a boy who likes to write poetry, but why is he making all this up between me and him?"

"Who says he is? He just says it's a poem *for* you, not *about* you."

"Cardmaker," I said, "why would he send me a love poem if it wasn't supposed to be *about* me?"

"Maybe he doesn't have anyone else to send it to."

I hadn't thought about that. I said, "It's still odd."

"Of course it's odd," Cardmaker said. "Everything that goes on around us is odd. We're not going to meet your simple hometown Buddy Goodboy over at Wales, any more than they're going to meet Nan Nice here at Charles. Don't you know by now we're all peculiar? Unwanted people are always peculiar."

"I'm not unwanted!" I almost shouted. "I told you that before!"

"You're in the way, and that's the same thing."

"Well, what about you?"

"I *wanted* to come to this dump," Cardmaker said, "but if I'd been all that wanted, I'd have been talked out of it. I'm from the extra-mouth-to-feed department."

"I still think Sumner Thomas is strange," I said.

"No one's disputing that," said Cardmaker, "but he has a lot of company, doesn't he?"

As we were coming away from shaking hands with Reverend Cunkle and lying about how much his sermon was enjoyed, APE reached out and grabbed Cardmaker, like some hungry jungle animal who'd been waiting all along for a weaker one to pounce on.

I heard Cardmaker say, "I'm *not* cold!"

"Well, then you are *not* well dressed, either! You cannot grab any vulgar combination you choose to, and prance across to worship dressed like—"

I had to keep walking; I could not hear any more.

I knew that Cardmaker was not wearing her winter coat because she'd outgrown it. Her wrists jumped way past the sleeves, and she could hardly button it. It was too short, as well, and the belt had been broken and patched half a dozen times.

I went back to Little Dorrit wondering whether or not I was becoming peculiar myself, as Cardmaker said, and if by any chance I was already peculiar, only didn't know it, while everyone else did and talked about me behind my back.

I was also trying to decide how to present myself as the planet Jupiter on Tuesday, for Miss Blue's Planet Day class. Everyone had her choice of being a planet, an imaginary form of life on one of the planets, or an astronaut who had just returned from a planet.

I had decided to be Jupiter. I was attracted by the

idea that it had twelve moons. I had spent a great deal of Friday afternoon in the library, reading up on Jupiter. It was the largest planet, too.

My father always said to dream on a grand scale. He would tell about a man in one of his groups who could never decide what he would wish for, if he could have only one wish. "I'd like my health," he'd reply. "No, wait! I'd like to see my son in Georgia," he'd continue. "No! I changed my mind. I'd rather make out with this woman in my office . . . or maybe come into money. I don't know!" My father said if he had learned to dream on a grand scale, he could have wished that in the best of health, on his way to see his son in Georgia, with the woman in his office accompanying him, he wins a fortune and discovers *all* his wishes will come true henceforth.

"Do you understand, Flan-Tan? Treat yourself to grand-scale dreams backed up by well-organized planning, and you can't fail!"

So I would be the biggest planet, Jupiter, with twelve moons, even though I had not answered my father's last letter and wasn't even sure any longer whether or not I cared to hear from him again.

As I arrived on David Copperfield, I saw the large space between Loretta Dow's teeth, and a finger. Loretta Dow was grimacing and indicating that I should be very quiet.

"Why?" I whispered.

"It's Miss Blue."

"What's wrong with her?"

"Shhhhhh. Dr. Ettinger is here."

There stood Billy, just outside Miss Blue's door. His

little bald head was cocked, and he was cupping his ear with one of his hands.

I went up to him. "Is she all right?"

"Hush, Flanders," he said. "Listen!"

Then I could hear it, very faintly, but very clearly: Miss Blue's voice, calling (chanting), "He that hath an ear, let him hear."

Loretta Dow pushed past me and said in an officious whisper, "Dr. Ettinger, I *do* believe she is hallucinating. I don't know if you remember, but every Wednesday I go to a psychiatrist in Richmond, and consequently I'm on the qui vive concerning most things psychological. She is definitely hallucinating, and it's not the first time."

Billy was dressed in an immaculate pin-striped suit, complete with the ubiquitous Phi Beta Kappa key. He looked up at me.

"Flanders, you're on David Copperfield nearly every day. Have you heard this before?"

I didn't have a chance to answer. Loretta Dow said, "It doesn't happen just on David Copperfield. She apparently chanted at dinner in Dombey and Son one evening. France Shipp told me."

I said, "She didn't chant. I was there."

"Well, she was reciting this same thing, Flanders."

"But she wasn't chanting," I said. I looked at Billy. "She doesn't chant. She doesn't bother anyone."

"She also announced that Jesus was in her room," Loretta said.

"I know about that," said Billy.

"She's very religious," I said.

"Flanders," said Loretta, hissing at me between her

teeth, "she's obviously ill if she's imagining that she was in the presence of Jesus."

"Were his disciples ill? What about all the saints?"

"Oh, yick, you're too preposterous," Loretta Dow said, and turned her attention back to Billy. "I *do* think Mrs. Ettinger should be given a full report on this, sir."

"Oh, yes, I'll tell her."

"She's not harming anyone," I said.

"*Yet*," Loretta Dow said.

"She never would."

"This has been in the making for some time," said Loretta Dow. "I've seen the symptoms developing; they were there last year."

"She's the best teacher at Charles," I said.

"Except for this little passion," said Loretta.

"So what, who doesn't have a passion? All the faculty do, if you ask me."

"Which nobody did!"

"How about Miss Mitchell and Miss Able?"

"Oh, shush, Flanders."

"And Miss Sparrow."

"Flanders, stay out of this."

"And Miss Balfour's passion with her own reflection."

"Girls," said Billy, "I don't think this discussion is necessary."

"And Miss Horton's passion for John Bob White!"

"That's a little different from having a passion for Jesus!"

"Different strokes for different folks!" I said.

"You're absurd," Loretta Dow said.

"You're narrow-minded," I said.

Billy said, "Girls! Girls!"

Then suddenly Miss Blue opened her door. "I thought I heard voices. Hello, Dr. Ettinger."

Billy bowed. "Hello, Miss Blue."

Her door wasn't open very wide, just wide enough to see the giant cross above her cot. Her room was neat and antiseptic-looking. She was wearing a black dress, and the usual silver cross.

"I missed church," she said. "I wasn't ill. Did you wonder where I was, was that it?" She frowned out at us, the flickering smile vanishing only to reappear, and her cheeks were flushed. The gardenia scent was very strong.

I said, "Yes, we were worried about you."

"I've been studying Revelations. Revelations 3:20."

"We thought we heard voices," Loretta Dow said. "Or at least one voice. Chanting."

"My voice," said Miss Blue. "I was repeating some of Revelations."

"Thank you," Billy said in his best gentleman's voice, bowing again. "We're happy to know you're feeling fine."

Loretta Dow said, "We wondered if Jesus was with you again."

I said quickly, "We did not."

Billy looked embarrassed.

Miss Blue said, "I don't think He was just now." She managed the flickering smile again. "You heard about it then?"

"Oh yes," Loretta said. "It's making the rounds."

Miss Blue looked slightly pleased and a little shy. "I don't know why me," she said.

"Why *not* you?" Loretta Dow said. "Who else?"

Miss Blue looked down at the floor modestly, her head shaking the way it did; she mumbled something which ended in "mysterious ways."

"We'd all better get ready for lunch," Billy said, pulling his gold chain from his vest pocket to study his watch. "It's getting late."

"I'll see you at your table, Miss Blue," I said.

She shook her head. "Not today, dear."

"Are you going out?"

"No, dear. I just think I'd better wait for Him."

I didn't say anything.

Billy cleared his throat nervously.

Loretta Dow said, "For Jesus?"

"Why yes."

"Why yes," Loretta Dow said. "Naturally. Of course."

During Quiet Hours that afternoon, I watched the teachers rushing off to The Caravan for a smoke and I listened to Agnes cleaning out her bureau drawers. It sounded like a horde of mice building nests in the walls.

I read some more about the planets, and Jupiter in particular, and I made sketches of a costume I was going to design for myself.

At one point I went across to my bookshelf and got down the Holy Bible. I had used Cardmaker's rules for remembering something. (Her home phone number was 324–2455; she remembered it by thinking: three times a twenty-four-year-old girl was raped by a twenty-four-year-old boy and a fifty-five-year-old man.)

I remembered: It was a revelation that three twenty-year-old girls were virgins.

Then I looked up Revelations 3:20.

Behold, I stand at the door and knock: if any man hear my voice, and open the door, I will come in to him, and will sup with him, and he with me.

I skimmed over the whole of Chapter 3, and saw that a few times this phrase was repeated: "He that hath an ear, let him hear."

Then I looked at the very fine print at the beginning of the chapter. I skipped from *2 The angel of the church of Sardis is reproved* to *15 The angel of Laodicea rebuked for being neither hot nor cold* to *20 Christ standeth at the door and knocketh.*

I remembered all her references to footsteps coming closer and divine knocks during her graces . . . and I remembered the day I knocked on her door and she called out that she was expecting me, without knowing who it was.

I was thinking about all of it when an envelope fell to the floor. I picked it up. There was writing on the outside.

If you are looking for something in the Holy Bible, make sure it isn't an easy answer. You will certainly find some soothing words as well as very cryptic and ambivalent meanings, affection as well as hostility, talk of peace and talk of war, not a lot about love between man and woman or marriage, and little about self-esteem.

If you are looking for a solution to your problems, look inside the envelope. There you will see all that you need.
With love from your father.

Inside I found a long narrow strip of cardboard with a slender mirror affixed to it.

Some time after light bell that evening, just after I had watched the lights go out on Tale of Two Cities, a note was shoved under my door. I read it by the light inside my closet.

Miss Blue has been asked to leave Charles School! She is to pack on Monday and leave early Tuesday morning. The official version will be that she has asked for a leave of absence and wants a rest. APE kicked her out. Atheists Against All Cruelty is going to take action. If you care to join us as a privileged outsider, report to Hard Times tomorrow after breakfast!

Fifteen

It was Cardmaker's idea.

Attending the after-breakfast session of Atheists Against All Cruelty were the three members: Cardmaker, Agnes, Sue Crockett; and the privileged outsider, me. We all agreed there was nothing we could do to change APE's decision. There wasn't enough time, for one thing; for another, none of our parents but Agnes' made any impression on APE. Cardmaker's father was the scapegoat of his diocese. Sue's mother was this merry widow who did little more than tool around in her white Mercedes all day. And my father was some kind of professional sex maniac.

Agnes was sitting on Cardmaker's bed trying not to sob. The noises she made when she cried were even worse than the ones she made when she snored. She would glance up at us with this face cracking from grief and moan "Ma Boooooo!" and Cardmaker would shake her hard and tell her to shut up.

"You're not even supposed to *be* here, Agnes!" Cardmaker tried to impress on her. "You're room campused! Now keep quiet!"

"I like the idea," Sue Crockett told Cardmaker, "but aren't there risks involved?"

The idea was that if we could not prevent this cruelty about to be inflicted on Miss Blue, we could at least soften it. Since it was so close to Christmas, we would present her with a gift from the school. No one but the four of us would know about it. One of us would steal official APE stationery for the note to accompany the gift. One of us would write the letter. The remaining two would procure the gift and place it outside Miss Blue's door.

The gift was to be the painting of Mary, Queen of Scots, which hung at the top of the stairs, just off David Copperfield.

Cardmaker asked Sue Crockett what risks she thought were involved.

"What if she goes to thank APE?"

"She won't," Cardmaker said. "For one thing, we'll wait until light bell rings before we place it outside her door and knock. She is *still* faculty chum for Little Dorrit. You know how literally she follows the rules. She won't leave David Copperfield. But for another thing, in the note from APE, we'll ask her to accept it without comment and as discreetly as possible, since no one else on the faculty is being remembered this year."

"Another thing," Sue Crockett said. "What will we put in the painting's place?"

"Nothing," Cardmaker said. "No one ever looks at that painting but Miss Blue."

"Herbert does," said Sue. Herbert was the school porter; he had been with Charles for twenty-nine years. "Herbert will notice."

"No," Cardmaker said. "We'll take the painting down at nine forty-five tonight. Miss Blue's train leaves at seven in the morning, so she'll be leaving the school at six thirty. No men, including Herbert, are allowed on dorm halls between seven and seven."

"What happens after seven? What happens tomorrow when it's found missing?" Sue said.

Cardmaker shrugged. "What can they prove?"

"They'll think it's been stolen," I said. "They'll think one of us is a kleptomaniac."

"Let *them* have a little pre-Christmas problem," said Cardmaker. "They sure laid one on Miss Blue!"

Agnes' face wrinkled up again and she began, "Ma Boooo," but Cardmaker put her hand over Agnes' mouth. "Cut it out!" she said. "Atheists aren't sentimental!"

It was decided that Sue Crockett would steal stationery from APE, since she was the only one of us not hall or room campused. Monday was an excellent day for such a theft, since it was the day off and there would be few girls or faculty members around. APE herself usually went for a drive with Billy, or stayed in their quarters on Tale of Two Cities.

Cardmaker would compose the note from APE and forge APE's name.

Agnes and I, because of our proximity to David Copperfield, would remove the painting from the wall, wrap it, and place it before Miss Blue's door. We would knock and run.

"So much for that," said Cardmaker. "Now on to official business. I'm sorry, Flanders, but you'll have to leave."

"Sure," I said getting up.

"Unless your eyes are finally opened."

"If I'm anything, I'm maybe an agnostic," I said.

"That's wishy-washy, spineless, and dull," said Cardmaker.

"That's what my mother says she is," said Sue Crockett. "She says it's safer that way. It's less offensive, in case there is a God."

"In case there is, *I* don't want to offend Him," I said.

"Or Her," Sue Crockett said. "My mother always says she doesn't want to offend Him *or Her*."

"A woman would never be God," Cardmaker said. "Not any God of *this* universe. Her maternal instincts would prevent it. She wouldn't be able to stand it! Only men like making war and money!"

"But my mother can sure spend it," Sue Crockett said.

"Sue," said Cardmaker, "how did a meeting of Atheists Against All Cruelty get turned into a discussion of your silly mother!"

"My mother isn't silly! Just because you're rich doesn't necessarily mean you're silly!"

"I've seen some pretty silly high Episcopalian ministers

in my time," said Cardmaker, "flouncing around in their handmade robes and their gold this and that, and they were all filthy rich!"

"How did a meeting of Atheists Against All Cruelty get turned into a discussion of High Episcopalian ministers?" Sue demanded angrily.

"So long," I said. "Since there won't be a Planet Day, I have to go back to Little Dorrit and destroy my design of a gown with twelve moons hanging off it."

"I was going to be Jupiter, too!" Cardmaker said.

I said, "It figures."

"Oz!" Agnes shouted.

"Write it down, don't talk," Cardmaker said. "I don't know how to translate, and someone will hear you, besides."

"Oz is probably Mars," I said. "She was going to be Mars."

Agnes came across to give me one of her pleased punches, but I got out the door before she could accomplish it.

On my way back to Little Dorrit, I thought of the empty seat at breakfast at the head of Miss Blue's table. According to the rumors, she had been told by APE last night after supper. The only time she had been seen since was after rising bell this morning when she went to locate Herbert, to ask him to bring up her trunk from the cellar.

Along Bleak House girls were adding their names to lists like "Shopping & a Soda," Movie & a Soda," "Nature Walk," "Horseback Riding," "Lunch & Shopping," et cetera. Each group was chaperoned by an E.L.A. member. By noon, there would be very few girls left in the school. I decided that I would ask Miss Blue if I could sit with her at lunch, that perhaps it would be a way of helping her face Dombey and Son; I would tell her we could walk down together when the lunch bell rang.

"Flanders Brown!"

APE's voice sent a current of shock through my system. I turned around and saw her standing down at the other end of Bleak House.

"I've been looking for you," she said.

She came stomping toward me, all in motion, the gold locket bouncing against her bosom, her spectacles bouncing across the bridge of her nose, her hair bouncing, her lower lip, all of her jumping around.

"What is it, ma'am?" I said.

She clamped her thick fingers across my thin wrist and backed me into a corner. "I want to speak privately, but I don't have time now to take you to my office, so we'll keep our voices lowered."

"Yes, ma'am."

"Where is Sumner Thomas?"

"He's at Wales Military Academy, Mrs. Ettinger."

"He has not been at Wales since yesterday noon. There is a search on for him, and your name has been brought into the matter, as someone he saw."

"I don't know anything about it, ma'am."

"If this is a prevarication and you do have information concerning his whereabouts, you will not go unpenalized, mark my word."

"Mrs. Ettinger, I don't know anything about it!"

"I *said* we were going to keep our voices lowered!"

"Yes, ma'am."

She loosened her grip on my skin; there were marks left.

"You have no Monday privileges until after Christmas, is that correct?"

"Yes, ma'am."

She seemed satisfied of something (of what? That I would not be free to escape the E.L.A. chaperone in town and rendezvous somewhere with Sumner Thomas?); she lumbered away, mumbling to herself.

When I arrived on David Copperfield, Miss Horton, Miss Sparrow, and Miss Balfour were all with Miss Blue. They were taking her to town for lunch. I caught only a fleeting glance of Miss Blue's face, shattered and pale, with eyes red from crying.

"Where will she go?" I asked Miss Sparrow, who had answered Miss Blue's door when I knocked. I whispered it, but Miss Sparrow answered me in a regular tone.

"New York, she says."

"New York City?"

"So she says."

"Does she have friends there?" I was trying to pull Miss Sparrow into the hall by speaking so low she would have to move forward to hear, but Miss Sparrow finally stopped in the doorway.

"I don't know," she said. "Have you made your bed yet, Flanders, or picked up your room?"

I hadn't. She knew I hadn't.

I said, "Just before Christmas. . . . I should think the faculty would protest to—"

Miss Sparrow cut me off. "Attend to your duties, Flanders."

Suddenly I felt very angry, and a little bold. "Does Reverend Cunkle know about this? Someone," I said pointedly, staring purposely at her new gold key, "ought to tell him."

The door shut in my face.

I felt like crying, like wailing, Ma Booo. Ma Boo. It hadn't even sunk in yet, and it wouldn't for a while, that Sumner Thomas had run away. I was too busy entertaining split-second images: the bathroom nail with O Bleeding Face hung on it; those blue eyes helplessly searching the faces in the dining room so many times on her way out, looking for some response; the thought of a young girl called Nesty with the boys after her, turning so soon into someone maybe crazy, maybe sick, maybe sane as I was, *or* APE; the soft little singsong tone that came from her so suddenly during the Thanksgiving dinner, "I talked to Jesus and He knew I knew He was there." I saw her reaching up to draw the heads of Marie Curie and Sir Ernest Rutherford, and I remembered the famous flickering smile when she said, "Cavendish called them noble gases because they wouldn't mix with any others. I call them the snobs."

I couldn't seem to get the smell of gardenia out of my nostrils all day, nor the sound of Miss Sparrow's voice telling me, "She's just a little over forty."

Dear Ernestine,
You cannot leave Charles School without taking some part of it, in appreciation for all that you've done for the girls. This is also a Christmas gift to you from all of us. Take it with you tomorrow morn-

ing and always enjoy it. (Please be discreet and don't comment on it, since we are not remembering other faculty members this year.)

*Sincerely,
Annie P. Ettinger*

We worried: Would she think it peculiar that such a personal note was typed, and not handwritten? (The written signature looked authentic.)

Would she be able to carry the painting *and* her hand luggage?

Agnes was in tears most of the afternoon, even though a bouquet of sweet peas had been delivered, with a card signed Stephen Woolwine. The only time I saw her face brighten was late that night shortly after we had lifted the painting from its hook and carried it carefully down to Little Dorrit.

"Dand!" She pointed to the small print under the words DEATH-CELL PRAYER OF MARY, QUEEN OF SCOTS *before she placed her head on the executioner's block. At the decree of her own cousin, also a woman.*

Keep us, oh God, from all smallness. Let us be large in thought, in word, and in deed. Let us have done with complaint, and leave off all self-seeking. May we put away all pretense, and meet each other with pity and without prejudice. May we never be hasty in judgment of others. Make us always generous. Let us take time to be calm and gentle. Teach us to put into action our better impulse and to walk unafraid. Grant that we may realize that the little things of life are those which create our differences, and that in the big things of life, we are as one under God. And, O Lord, let us never forget to be kind. Amen.

From her room on A Christmas Carol, Sue Crockett

saw Miss Blue leave the following morning at twenty minutes to seven. Ahead of her, Herbert was carrying her hand luggage into the waiting taxi. Miss Blue managed to carry her gift all by herself, though it was almost as large as she was. Then it was tied to the roof of the taxi, and by six forty-five, Miss Blue and her gift were speeding off to catch a train north.

We soon learned that on her way out she had left a note in APE's box thanking her for her generosity. APE found it there sometime after breakfast. Not long after she found it, right in the middle of the school day, the bells seemed to go berserk, ringing off schedule, relentlessly ringing CLANG—DONG DONG, CLANG—DONG DONG, CLANGDONG, CLANGDONGCLANG, like someone who had gone soft in the head was suddenly pulling the rope herself.

It was APE, calling for an unprecedented emergency assembly, immediately!

Sixteen

The painting of Mary, Queen of Scots, in her death cell had been donated to Charles School by The Alumnae Association. The artist was a member of the class of 1900. The painting was therefore "priceless," although it was insured for a thousand dollars.

Before APE's investigation of Miss Blue's "gift" was concluded, nearly everyone at the school, including Herbert, had been grilled in her office.

When it was Agnes' turn, APE placed a pad of yellow-lined paper between them, tore off the top sheet and scratched across it, "Did Carolyn Cardmaker have anything to do with this?"

Agnes read the message, thought a moment, then picked up the pen in front of her and wrote back, "What?"

APE began rubbing her diamond and moaning. "Agnes,"

APE wrote across another piece of paper, "I am sick in bed with a doctor at the change that has come over you, at the impudence, disrespect, and chicanery!"

There was no point in punishing her; all privileges had been suspended, including those extended to the Extra Lucky Asses. Until the guilty were unmasked, the innocent would suffer.

A pall hung over the school that even the approach of Christmas vacation couldn't lift. Everyone was testy and trigger-tempered, many of us suffering from sugar insufficiency since The Sweet Shoppe was closed as well.

When it was announced that the annual Christmas party was to be canceled, Cardmaker told us she was going to confess.

"Let me take the rap for the whole thing," she said. "Why should all of us pay? It was my idea anyway."

Sue Crockett said that it was very brave of Cardmaker and gave her a hug of relief.

Agnes and I filed in after her when she went to APE's office to turn herself in. About ten minutes later, Sue appeared, too.

When APE became coherent, it was decided that the family of each girl who was responsible would immediately wire the school two hundred and fifty dollars, which would be kept in escrow until the painting was recovered. (Miss Blue had left no forwarding address, but had announced she would write when she was settled.)

Cardmaker insisted she intended to "resign permanently" from Charles School, and that there was no point in approaching her father for any two hundred and fifty dollars! Cardmaker began loudly proclaiming her atheism, at the same time noisily questioning APE about what kind of a religious school was it that believed communication with Jesus Christ was a sign of mental instability?

On December 19th, a few days before the beginning of Christmas vacation, Cardmaker was expelled. She was made to leave that day. Her presence was considered a poisoning influence on the student body.

Cute and I helped her carry down her bags. She was wearing that same flimsy corduroy jacket over a nylon dress, even though it was in the twenties out.

"What are you crying for, Cute?" she said. "Isn't a good Baptist glad to see an atheist getting her come-uppance?"

Cute said, "When you knock the nose, the eye hurts."

Cardmaker hugged her hard, and that made me start crying.

"If you go to Auburn for Christmas, come see me in Union," she said to me. "Promise?"

Near dusk, she was hustled out the side entrance just below Little Dorrit. Something like the sound of a trapped coyote dying came from above. It was Agnes waving and wailing, and for the first time Cardmaker's face gave, too, and the tears streamed down her cheeks as she followed Herbert to the taxi.

Seventeen

I arrived at Penn Station on the 21st of December around three in the afternoon. The bus I had to catch for Newark airport didn't leave until eight that night. My father had advised me to walk directly into the Statler Hilton, and to pass the time in the lobby, in view of the registration desk. I could sit in one of the comfortable chairs and read, or do some of the homework I wouldn't want to do after I arrived at Grandma Brown's in Auburn.

Instead, I took a taxi down to 58 West 9th Street.

I kept rereading the list of names under the bells in the entrance. Finally I realized that

Deacon/Brown

was one person: Ruth Deacon Brown, my mother. I had almost forgotten her maiden name, since she had never used it after she married my father. She was always Ruth Karen Brown.

I rang the bell and waited nervously for an answering buzzer to admit me inside the apartment building. There was no response. I tried again, then tried the door, then paced around anxiously trying to decide what I'd do next.

I pressed the Superintendent's bell, and the buzzer rang instantly.

Once I was inside, a thin young man smoking a pipe appeared in the doorway of a ground-floor apartment.

"I'm Ruth Deacon Brown's daughter," I said.

"What do you want, a medal for that?"

"I just want to wait in her apartment, if that's possible."

"I don't know no Ruth Brown."

"Ruth Deacon?"

"Miss Deacon? Yeah, but she ain't got no daughter your age. She ain't got no daughter, period, that I know about."

"Why would I lie?"

"Why do pigs whistle, miss? Don't waste my time. Miss Deacon's at work."

"Where?"

"You're her daughter but you don't know where she works? Cute."

"I am her daughter," I said.

"I'm her nephew, miss; I'm her great-grandpa. But I don't go inside her apartment when she ain't home."

"Can I wait here in the lobby?"

"Free country." He ducked back inside his apartment and shut the door.

There were no chairs in the lobby. It wasn't a very pretty lobby, just one table with some mail on it, and a chain attached to the table leg and fixed to the wall, so no one could drag the table away.

I stood around for about three quarters of an hour before the superintendent poked his head out again. He shoved a straight-backed wooden kitchen chair out to me and said I could take a load off my feet.

Nearly two hours later I saw my mother step inside the lobby.

I had forgotten how much I looked like her, how familiar she was to me.

She looked at me as though she had just been punched hard and was trying to stay on her feet; and although her mouth opened, for a moment she couldn't seem to make a sound.

I said, "Hello."

"Flan! Flan!" She walked over to me and hugged me, and even though I was fighting to keep from crying, I somehow couldn't hug her back, and I wanted to escape her embrace. She sensed it and backed off.

"Have you been waiting long, Flan?"

"A little over two hours."

She punched the elevator button and the door opened. We went inside.

"Why didn't you let me know you were coming?"

"I didn't know myself."

"Are you on Christmas vacation?"

"I'm on my way to Grandma Brown's."

"I'm so glad you came, Flan! I was working."

"Where?"

"I work over at New York University."

"Oh," I said. "Where Bobby is."

"He teaches there. I work there and attend classes."

We got off the elevator on the eleventh floor.

153

Her apartment was very small: one long, narrow room, with a tiny kitchenette. The furniture was shabby, and there were heavy drapes across the window, which made the atmosphere kind of seedy and dark.

She seemed really pleased, though, and she said, "It's a real steal. Two hundred and fifty a month!"

I tried to manage something like "swell," but it came out, "Well—"

She took my coat and while she was hanging it up she said, "I can walk to work. Isn't that fantastic? No crowded subways or buses for me!"

I didn't say anything. She had wall-to-wall carpeting but there were holes in it, and it was practically worn through at one point near the door.

"There are some wonderful inexpensive little restaurants nearby, and the Village is very lively. Fun."

"Great," I said.

"There's a marvelous Gothic-type old library practically across the street. The New School is close by. We've got trees and flower boxes, did you notice how pretty the street is? And I'm told that last summer some people even planted corn a few doors down."

I said, "Where does he live?"

"Who's he?"

"Bobby."

"Bobby lives on Washington Square Park."

"How come?"

"How come what?"

"Nothing."

"What?"

"Nothing," I said. "I just wondered why he doesn't live . . . closer."

"Washington Square Park isn't far."

"I mean much closer to you, or with you, or something."

"Oh, that," she said. "That wasn't much, Flan."

"It wasn't much?"

"No, it wasn't."

"Oh," I said. "I thought it was. I mean, it broke up our home, I mean, maybe it wasn't much, but—"

"It didn't break up our home, Flan."

"That's news to me. I think it's news to Dad, too."

"Sit down, Flan."

"I don't have to be sitting down all the time, do I?"

"No," she said, sitting down herself, lighting a cigarette. "I just thought you might like to be comfortable."

"I've been *sitting down* in the lobby for hours!"

"Flan, you didn't let me know you were coming. I have a job."

"I don't care," I said. "I did a lot of thinking while I was waiting."

"About what, Flan?"

"Personal stuff," I said. "Stuff that involves my personal life!"

"All right," she said. "I won't pry."

"It isn't that you're prying. It's just that I'm into a lot of things you don't know anything about."

"I wanted to write you. Your father said you didn't want to hear from me."

"If Bobby Santanni isn't important, what are you doing in New York?"

"I didn't say he wasn't important. I said *it* wasn't, whatever we had wasn't. He's still a dear friend."

"I don't give a damn about Bobby Santanni!" I said. "I didn't come here to talk about Bobby Santanni!"

"Flan, I left your father because I want to be someone in my own right."

"And because you hated what he forced you to do?"

"Flan, what are you talking about?"

"The television show. The stuff that James Tripp said about you and Dad."

"Your father never forced me to do anything."

"It sounded like you had all these orgies or something."

"There were no orgies, I promise you."

"I don't know what to think about anything anymore," I said. "If you wanted to be someone in your own right, why didn't you think of that before you had me?"

"I wasn't adult enough yet."

"You were over 21."

"Age has nothing to do with it. I might as well have been thirteen years old when I had you."

"But you had me!" I said. "I arrived. I'm here. You should have thought of all this other stuff before."

"Flan, I have news for you," said my mother, grinding out her cigarette in the ashtray. "I didn't give up my right to individuality once I had you."

I thought about it. I shrugged. "I don't know." I walked across and sat down on the couch opposite her.

"Flan?"

"What?"

"You're going to meet a very old person one day. And when you do, you're going to have only her to answer to, and only her to be responsible to, and only her to look back with and decide what it was all about with . . . and that old person is yourself. I hope you'll be prepared for her."

"That's hairy," I said. "Hairy and heavy."

"But it's true."

"You'll probably send her to bed with a heart attack looking back on your thing with Bobby and God knows what else that went on right under our roof."

"Your father is an experimenter, Flan."

"How do I explain that? People see a show like *Controversy*; how do I explain what they heard, by saying my father is an experimenter?"

"You don't explain it," she said.

"I sure don't! Not even to myself!"

"He's doing what he believes in. Now I'm doing what *I* believe in. What about you?"

"I don't know," I said. "I'm not an atheist. I was French-kissed this fall and I wanted to go home and boil my mouth."

My mother smiled. "What else?"

"I don't know."

"Well, that's a start. You're not an atheist and so far you don't take to French kissing. . . . What about this asthma that began last summer?"

"I have a single room because of it. It hasn't been bad, just two big attacks. But I had to room on Little Dorrit because of it, and Little Dorrit is where Number Fours room. That's how I met Agnes!"

"Who's she?"

Well, I told her everything, all about life at Charles School, ending with Dad's wiring the two hundred and fifty with the message "There'd better be a good explanation for this!"

There was a lot to tell her, too, which astonished me because I'd only been at Charles for three months. But there was a whole little world to tell about, and it was like any world, with things that were hilarious and sad and crazy and unbelievable.

We were really laughing, and when my mother suddenly cried out that it was seven past seven, and I hadn't eaten, and I had to be at the East Side air terminal by eight, I couldn't believe the time had passed so fast. But something else: I couldn't believe all that I had to tell, all that I'd seen and heard and been a part of, and for the first time in my life, I'd been and seen and heard on my own. Do you see what I mean?

I think my mother did.

She rode all the way to Newark with me on the bus. Before I boarded the plane, she put out her hand. "You're still my little girl," she said, "but you're very much your own girl now, too, aren't you?"

I hugged her good-bye.

It's always snowing in Upstate New York near Christmas, and that night was no exception. The plane landed in Syracuse, and through a blinding snowstorm with the wind cutting across the open spaces, I could see my father standing by the gate waiting with my grandmother.

I had the loneliest feeling in the world then: that feeling that just when everything was really working out for you, you remembered someone things were really bad for, and your insides went numb.

"Merry Christmas!" my father shouted.

"Merry Christmas!" my grandmother shouted.

I whispered at the storm, "Miss Blue, are you okay?"

I knew the answer was no.

Eighteen

Christmas at Grandma Brown's was okay. I saw Carol MacLean and some of my old friends. Carol repeated what she'd written to me about my mother, that in her opinion my mother was supercourageous to run off with a younger man. I didn't bother straightening her out on the subject because I don't think Carol would understand that my mother didn't run off with anyone. She just wanted out.

If my father couldn't understand it, or even believe it, why should Carol?

"I certainly hope Bobby didn't ditch her," said my father when I told him she wasn't living with Bobby. She wasn't even interested in him that way, anymore.

"I don't think he did. I think what she told me is the truth. She wants to have her own life," I said.

"Well, what the hell did she have all these years if it wasn't her own life?"

"Your life?" I suggested.

He pretended not to hear. He said, "She's probably a lot more involved with Santanni than she let on to you."

I think my father had to believe that for his ego's sake. When you think about it, it's funny, isn't it? He would rather believe that his wife left him for another man than believe that she just wanted another way of life, independent of his.

My grandmother's comment was, "Many women can't resist Italian men. I've seen it in the movies." (My grandmother always pronounced Italian "eyetalian.")

My father sulked a lot over the holidays, not just because of what I'd told him about my mother, but also because once he heard the whole story of Miss Blue's "gift," he gave up all hope of ever seeing the two hundred and fifty dollars again.

"That painting's probably in a New York City hock shop right now!" he grumbled.

"I don't know where it is, but I know she wouldn't hock it."

"I'm not saying your Miss Blue would hock it. I'm saying the fellow who got it off her would!"

"Don't," I said.

New Year's Eve afternoon, I arrived in Union, to spend the evening and following day with Cardmaker. Then I would return to Charles School.

Cardmaker seemed to be sulking, too.

"Isn't there *some* way your father could get you back in school?" I said.

"I don't want to go back there. I don't have the clothes for that place. I barely get by in a hole like Union, never mind competing with that bunch."

"Is your father going to be transferred?"

"That's what we hear. We don't know where."

"It's a lousy Christmas for you," I said.

"Oh, I can take anything," Cardmaker said, "or almost anything. I can take just about anything."

"Except what?"

"Nothing," she said.

"You don't want to talk about it?"

"It's nothing. It's just my father. He's trying to outsmart me," she complained.

At that point Mrs. Cardmaker announced that dinner was on the table, and four little Cardmakers rushed down the stairs, followed by Cardmaker's father and Cardmaker and me.

We were all wearing heavy sweaters because the wind came right through the rickety walls in the dining room. Before anyone picked up a fork, Reverend Cardmaker said, "Atheists are not required to bow their heads during grace."

Cardmaker's elbow jabbed into my side. "See what I mean about him?" she whispered.

"Did you tell him *I* was one?" I whispered back.

Reverend Cardmaker said, "We thank thee, O Lord, for blessing us again with good food, good company, and goodwill in our hearts. Amen."

Dinner was baked beans and franks and homemade brown bread.

"Cardmaker," I whispered as the four little Cardmakers began a lot of noise at the other end of the table, "did you tell him I was an atheist?"

"I didn't say you were or you weren't. Besides, you said you were an agnostic. There's not much difference in his eyes."

"I said I was maybe an agnostic."

"That's the trouble with you agnostics," Cardmaker said. "You're so damn wishy-washy and jelly-spined. Maybe this and maybe that."

Reverend Cardmaker spoke up then. He was a thin, tall man with very dark brown eyes and a perpetual little tip to his lips, as though he was always on the verge of telling a funny story.

"We're having our annual New Year's Eve service this evening, Flanders, and of course you're invited, unless attending church is against your principles."

"*I'm* not an atheist," I said.

"She's maybe an agnostic," Cardmaker said.

"I'm probably not even that," I said. "It's not against my principles to go to church."

"That's very encouraging news," said Reverend Cardmaker.

After dinner I helped Cardmaker with the dishes.

"Why did you tell him about being an atheist?"

"APE told him."

"I never understood why you told APE."

"I wanted to be expelled," she said. "Two hundred and fifty dollars is a real bundle to my father!" She put the dish towel around her head like a scarf, and held a spoon up to her eye like a monocle. Then in this falsetto voice she said, *"O sancta simplicitas!"*

We both laughed.

By seven forty-five, everyone was leaving for the church, which was just across the street. I decided to stay with Cardmaker, and we got out the Scrabble board and tuned the radio to a rock station.

"I'd rather listen to something softer," I said.

Cardmaker said, "I wouldn't. The louder the better."

I made the word *flower* and waited for Cardmaker to take her turn.

She said, "I didn't go at Christmas, either."

"Go where?"

"To church."

"Did everyone else go?"

"Of course, dummy!"

"Well, I don't belong to a very religious family. How would I know?"

"We always go. We all sit in a long row together!"

I said, "It's your turn."

The church bells began to ring.

I said, "It's your turn, Cardmaker."

"I heard you the first time."

The bells were louder, and they began to play "O Come, All Ye Faithful."

Cardmaker made the word *so*.

I made *lambent*.

"That's not a word!" Cardmaker said.

I said, "It means lightly flickering. Look it up."

"It's not a word anybody's heard about!"

"It's a word, though."

"No one ever uses it. You should only use words people use."

"It's in the dictionary," I said. "Play!"

She was biting her lip, actually chewing on it.

"Play," I said. "It's your turn."

"I can't think with those damn bells. Turn up the radio."

"I can't think with the radio turned up any louder!" I said. "Why don't you just go and get it over with!"

"Because he said he didn't want me going just to go. He said if I was going just to go, not to."

"If you want to go, go."

"He said if I wanted to thank God for last year and put in one of my long and unreasonable lists of requests for next year, all well and good, but if I didn't believe in God, it would just be wasted energy and very much against his own conservationist principles."

"Well, what are we going to do?" I said. "We're not playing Scrabble."

"I'm trying to think of a word," she said. "I don't have any vowels."

"How long are those bells going to ring?" I said.

"Until everyone gets there."

"How long is that?"

"HOW DO I KNOW!" Cardmaker shouted, and knocked the Scrabble board away from in front of her, scattering the pieces across the room.

I didn't say anything.

"I'm sorry," Cardmaker said.

I said, "Why don't you go?"

"And take God back?" Cardmaker said, the way someone asks something they want to hear a yes answer to.

I nodded.

"Let's go!" Cardmaker shouted.

When I got back to Charles School, there was a letter from Butler Peabody.

Dear Flanders,
You were probably aware of my arrangement with Carolyn Cardmaker whereby we both benefited from invitations to our respective social events. With Carolyn absent now and also in the absence of Sumner Thomas (he has received permission from his father to enlist in the United States Army) I thought we might effect a similar arrangement. May I know your feelings in this regard?
B.P.

I replied,

Dear B.P.
The whole deal sounds too greasy to suit me, under the circumstances.
F.B.

I don't know what exactly I meant by that, but the thought of us dancing around together while Cardmaker was back in Union and Sumner was marching around some army post just reminded me of something someone would do who wore his hair close to his scalp, slicked down and shiny.

Sometimes at night when I couldn't sleep, I'd think of Sumner, and the poems he sent me, and the note his mother left, and I'd know the poems were written to his mother. I'd know he needed the army because the army would really tell him what to do with his life, for the rest of his life, because he was lost.

In the morning I'd think maybe I was all wrong. Maybe he just liked writing poems and maybe he just liked dressing up in uniforms, and maybe it didn't make any sense to try and analyze everything. Where had it ever gotten my father? My father hadn't even known his own wife wanted out.

France Shipp didn't return after Christmas vacation. There were rumors circulating that she was pregnant. But Peter Rider was back at Wales, as handsome as ever, showing no signs of being involved in anything like that. ... We never knew the truth. France didn't write anyone, didn't visit, was never heard from again after her roommate packed her trunk and Herbert wheeled it away to be shipped to her.

Agnes learned more about Stephen Woolwine. He was a fifty-year-old man who kept over a hundred dogs in his house. His name was in all the newspapers when the city voted to rezone his neighborhood and force him out. He was a bachelor and a scrap collector. The only place he visited (except for his junk-collecting missions) was St. Thomas Episcopal Church, which he attended faithfully every Sunday. The ASPCA took his dogs and Stephen Woolwine went to Richmond to live with a brother. His correspondence with Agnes ended abruptly with his notoriety.

The big news was that a man took Miss Blue's place. He was a young man in his early twenties, the only man ever in residence at Charles School. Mr. Leogrande became our faculty chum, too, living on David Copperfield, but going to the john two flights down on Great Expectations.

He was a terrible teacher; he made science about as colorful as a sack of flour. But he had other things in his favor: He was a man, and he was nearer our age than the other faculty members. He had sex appeal, according to Agnes (My grandmother would not have been surprised that anyone named Ernesto Leogrande had sex appeal!) and for a while Agnes grew thin and was alternately weepy and giggly, and always on one subject: HIM.

Mr. Leogrande convinced Agnes to attend our Valentine dance, instead of putting herself in the infirmary as she always did. It was her first dance, and APE let Mr. Leogrande escort her to it.

The ice was broken after that. Agnes went to all the dances, but not with Mr. Leogrande.

What was it about those years that made young Italians pant after older women? Mr. Leogrande fell under Miss Sparrow's spell. I looked out toward The Caravan one Sunday afternoon and saw them in a pouring rain, huddled under Miss Sparrow's cape, which she was still wearing, walking as though it was a sunny summer day.

Sundays in church we looked for signs of tragedy, potential suicide, or homicide across the face of Reverend Cunkle. There were those who swore that there were new wrinkles and dark circles under his eyes from sleepless nights, and once in Sweet Shoppe Queue I was told by Ditty Hutt that Reverend Cunkle had cried in his wife's lap, while she patted his bald head and told him, "Edward, there was no way for it to end happily."

Agnes went to all the dances including the May Day

dance. I don't remember who her date was that time. Mine was John Dowder. Cute had planned it for months, knowing how I carried on about John ever since that Sunday when we all went out to dinner together.

He was exactly as I remembered him, as handsome, maybe more.

I don't remember now what it was he said, what gross thing it was that made me cringe and blush and wish someone would cut his tongue out so he would just be there to look up at and lean against. It turned out not to be important. After his first dance with Agnes, anything about him that I didn't like wasn't going to have anything to do with me, anyway.

"Perfect match!" Cardmaker wrote after I wrote her the news. "Two great faces until they open their big mouths!"

One night near the end of the year, I went into Miss Mitchell's room to ask permission to be excused from gym.

"Will we see you next year, Flanders?"

Sticking out from the edge of her desk blotter, I saw the picture of Miss Able pieced together and Scotch-taped. She had recovered it from the wastebasket where I had tossed it along with pieces of my father's letter.

"I suppose I'll be back," I said.

"You only suppose?"

"It's hard to be certain of much."

I'd learned that in a year's time at Charles School. Boarding school is like a little world, with all the lessons of the large one taught in minuscule.

The painting of Mary, Queen of Scots, was never recovered. It seemed fitting that it should be gone along with Miss Blue, the only one who would really have missed it.

People drop out of your life, some by accident, some by will, some by default: France Shipp, Sumner, Miss Blue . . . and some mean more and some mean less.

I never graduated from Charles School. In my junior year I went to live with my mother in New York City. I went to school there. Agnes wrote faithfully the news of Charles School. Some summers when I went up to Auburn, I stopped in Union to see Cardmaker, whose father had managed to fight the bishop and keep that parish.

I thought I'd never lose track of Cardmaker and Agnes, but I did. We lost track of each other, stopped writing. Cardmaker was marrying someone from Union when last heard of; Agnes was in her final year of Sweet Briar.

Eventually I even stopped wondering about them, where they were, what they were doing. Other people took their places and ultimately others took theirs. Time passed and few stayed and there were always more to come.

But I never forgot Miss Blue. I'm not sure why. I think of her every time I walk the streets of New York City. I try to imagine her way back that Christmas season, a tiny figure wearing a large cross, carrying a huge picture, enveloped by the tall skyscrapers and the onrushing crowds, making her way along somehow. Then I have to stop imagining, for the city is too cruel to the likes of a Miss Blue. I can never look in the window of a pawnshop for fear one day I'll see the painting of Mary, Queen of Scots, and beside it Miss Blue's huge cross.

Sometimes when I pass a church I hear that tiny singsong voice repeating, "I talked to Jesus and He knew I knew He was there," and I wonder all over again why she always smelled of gardenia, why that particular scent, and what she had been like when she was "Nesty." How had she gotten from "Nesty" to our Miss Blue? Could it happen to anyone? To me? And what would it take to make it happen?

There are never any answers to these mysteries. But I still have a daydream that sometime I might come upon her. She was only around forty and she wouldn't be that much older now.

In my daydreams she suddenly appears—in the half-light of early evening along Fifth Avenue in the forties . . . or in the Christmas crowds on a snowy morning outside Macy's . . . at the back of a small restaurant, the kind that serves hot popovers and fresh-baked homemade bread . . . or on a city park bench in a circle of sun on a cold afternoon.

I see the light blue eyes look up—remembering the times I would see them trying to connect with someone else's on the way out of Dombey and Son.

Our eyes meet. I smile. Does she recognize me, or remember me at all?

"Miss Blue," I say. "It's me. Is it really you?"

THE END